Next Steps
with
Academic
Conversations

Next Steps with Academic Conversations

New Ideas for Improving Learning Through Classroom Talk

Jeff Zwiers

Stenhouse
PUBLISHERS

Portsmouth, New Hampshire

www.stenhouse.com

Library of Congress Cataloging-in-Publication Data

Names: Zwiers, Jeff, author.
Title: Next steps with academic conversations : new ideas for improving learning through classroom talk / Jeff Zwiers.
Description: Portsmouth, New Hampshire : Stenhouse Publishers, [2019] | Includes bibliographical references. | Summary: "This title examines the benefits and practices of academic conversations and social discourse in grades 3-12. Builds on activities and why academic conversations are important"— Provided by publisher.
Identifiers: LCCN 2019012945 | ISBN 9781625312990 (paperback) | ISBN 9781625313003 (ebook)
Subjects: LCSH: Communication in education. | Interaction analysis in education. | Teacher-student relationships.
Classification: LCC LB1033.5 .Z954 2019 | DDC 371.102/2—dc23 LC record available at https://lccn.loc.gov/2019012945

Cover design, interior design, and typesetting by Lucian Burg,
LU Design Studios, Portland, ME

Manufactured in the United States of America

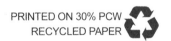

PRINTED ON 30% PCW
RECYCLED PAPER

25 24 23 22 21 20 19   9 8 7 6 5 4 3 2 1

Contents

Acknowledgments

To all the great educators with whom I have had the opportunity to work and collaborate, I would like to thank you. Special thanks go to Theresa Blanchard, Leslee Cybulski, Magda Chia, Gil Diaz, Jack Dieckmann, Anastasia Difino, Vinci Daro, Gabriel Enriquez, Sue Fotopoulos, Maria Friedland, Claude Goldenberg, Dania Ghrawi, Kenji Hakuta, Sara Hamerla, Bonnie Hansen, Tara House, Patrick Hurley, Nicole Knight, Nancy Ku, Annie Kuo, Catherine O'Connor, David Pearson, Gina Ramirez, Tonya Ward Singer, Kristin Stout, and Steven Weiss.

Introduction

Speech has allowed the communication of ideas, enabling human beings to work together to build the impossible. Mankind's greatest achievements have come about by talking, and its greatest failures by not talking. It doesn't have to be like this. Our greatest hopes could become reality in the future. With the technology at our disposal, the possibilities are unbounded. All we need to do is make sure we keep talking.

—*Stephen Hawking*

This book is meant for teachers who want a streamlined, practical guide to beefing up the quality and quantity of productive conversations in their lessons. For those of you who are familiar with conversation skills and have dabbled in their development already, this is a resource to inspire and support your next steps on this journey.

Since the publication of *Academic Conversations: Classroom Talk That Fosters Critical Thinking and Content Understandings* (Zwiers and Crawford 2011), I have worked with many teachers who, with some hard work and creativity, have succeeded in developing their students' conversation skills and using conversations to foster growth in content understandings, thinking skills, and language. This book builds on the original ideas in *Academic Conversations*, offering (a) an updated synthesis of conversation work in classrooms,

(b) highlights of recent classroom-based research and theory on classroom conversation, (c) answers to questions that have emerged during conversation work, and (d) new classroom strategies and practices for fostering classroom conversations.

In most classrooms, high-quality conversations between students are still rare, especially in settings with students from diverse linguistic and cultural backgrounds. Why? Because, too often, these students tend to receive more basic, direct, and boring types of instruction. Conversation-rich teaching is a radical and, for many, risky approach to learning. In the minds of many educators, such teaching does not have enough direct influence on test scores. And yet, conversation was not invented to help people choose the right answers on tests. Conversation evolved to solve problems, build ideas, build relationships, and understand others, and improve the world.

As a result of more and better conversations, test scores might go up or down. If they change just a little, you might feel that the differences aren't worth the effort. Yet most teachers with whom I have worked have seen growth in engagement, content learning, language, *and* even test scores. If your primary focus is not test scores, and you have additional and higher priorities for students (such as stronger relationships, graduating from high school, interest in learning, ability to converse with a wide range of others, empathy, collaborative argument skills, critical thinking, and creativity), then this book and its ideas should be worth your time.

Chapter 1 describes the core conversation skills to be developed during lessons. Chapter 2 covers what it means to build ideas in conversations, given that many students—and adults—don't yet understand what building an idea with another person entails. Chapter 3 then describes how to foster students' collaborative, as opposed to competitive, argumentation skills. Chapter 4 covers discipline-specific conversation strategies and how to develop effective conversation prompts across grade levels and subject areas. Chapter 5 describes formative and summative assessment practices that help teachers and students see growth and what to work on next. And Chapter 6 covers the vital steps needed to cultivate a classroom culture of conversation.

Because classroom conversation is such a big and important topic, I also encourage you to use the wide range of other resources that focus on classroom talk. You can search online for *classroom discourse, dialogic learning, accountable talk, collaborative argumentation,* and *thinking together,* and you will likely see important names such as Courtney Cazden, Martin Nystrand, James Gee, Neil Mercer, and others. You will find most of their resources listed in the back of this book.

Last, thank you for taking the time and energy to improve the conversational learning of your students. The conversation work that you do will make profound differences in your students' lives. Also, as you read the following chapters and try new strategies in your classroom, please share your insights and reflections with others so that conversation-rich learning deepens across grade levels and disciplines.

Chapter 1

Academic Conversations

Conversations are ships, anchors,
and destinations.

Academic conversations are powerful ways to develop students' content understandings, thinking skills, and language. But they are much more than just tools for learning. Regardless of the topic, students need to adeptly use conversations, whether or not they are "academic," to overcome a wide range of life's challenges and to build relationships, empathy, and social skills. While this book tends to focus on conversations in school, the core skills emphasized in this and other chapters are helpful outside of school as well. In fact, you probably know some adults who need to work on several (or all) of these skills.

An academic conversation changes something in the minds of its participants. Typically, this thing is academic in nature, but it doesn't have to be. Most often, changes happen when ideas, information, or values are strengthened, weakened, clarified, chosen, or otherwise transformed. For example, a fifth-grade student conversed with her partner about the theme of a novel that they had read. She shared a possible theme, and her partner shared a similar theme but with different evidence and applications. The students worked together to clarify terms and combine evidences. These students each walked away with a much more developed idea that they collaboratively built up through conversation. Every conversation, in fact, should build at least one idea, and participants should walk away a little different—with more knowledge, a changed perspective, more conviction, or a new way to solve a problem. Chapter 2 provides an in-depth look at this building process and how to foster it in student conversations.

Benefits of Academic Conversations

Academic conversations offer many benefits to students. You likely already know these, but, given that it does take quite a bit of work to use and improve conversations throughout the school day, it doesn't hurt to be reminded of them.

- *Content learning.* Conversations offer a chance for students to share their questions and confusions with others. Not every partner will be able to clarify everything, but conversation does allow students to get a better idea of what they don't know and what they need to know. As they talk with partners, they also benefit from the knowledge, evidence, and experiences of others. For example, they might have missed something in the text that a conversation partner helps to fill in. And, as you will see throughout this book, conversations empower students to build their own robust ideas related to the discipline. When you build an idea, the idea and the thinking and language that were used to build it last longer in the brain than if students had memorized a bunch of disconnected words or rules.

- *Language development.* Every other turn in an authentic conversation, the student receives oral input tailored just for him or her. If, let's say, Ana is talking with David about the theme of a story, and she doesn't understand something that David just said, she says, "What?" or "Huh?" Then, David rephrases, uses a synonym, acts it out, or does whatever it takes to help Ana understand what he is saying. And every other turn, Ana is pushed to put her ideas into words and sentences (oral output) for David to understand and use in building his ideas. As she constructs meaning, the words and grammar tend to stick in her brain. And some words and grammatical structures are reinforced because they are used multiple times in the conversation.

- *Stronger socio-emotional skills.* In the Bantu language, the word *ubuntu* means that a person becomes a person only through other people. Conversations play a large role in this process. Neuroscientists argue that our brains and minds are shaped by face-to-face interactions with other people. Rather than just decoding and encoding verbal messages during conversation (as robots might do), a person's mind tries to understand, or mirror, the other's mind by inferring meanings, feelings, and values (Hari and Kujala 2007). As students converse with others, they see

how others think and feel about a range of issues and how they express
those feelings. This builds the ability to understand how others view
and respond to the world, which leads to the important skill of empathy.
Empathy in turn allows people to connect with others and create better
relationships. If, for example, when you talk, I rarely understand where
you are coming from, it is less likely that you will be my friend. Lack of
empathy and other social skills, as we see often in the news, can lead to
major misunderstandings and problems in the world.

- *Stronger academic identity, agency, and voice.* Many students, for a
  variety of reasons, do not feel that they are "academic" or that they can
  learn as well as their peers. Conversations can help build an academic
  identity. When students are given the freedom to work together to build
  up ideas and ways of expressing those ideas, their sense of agency in
  their learning grows. Agency means, in a nutshell, that you learn to use
  the tools of learning (language, thinking, etc.) to do meaningful things,
  rather than just to show that you can use the tools. (Would you rather
  use tools to construct a house or be tested on your use of tools on pieces
  of scrap wood year after year?) Students also tend to feel that they
  have more of a voice: that their ideas matter and can contribute to the
  collective learning and ideas in class. These things, of course, help build
  students' sense of belonging, confidence, and the knowledge that they
  can learn just as well as others in class, in school, and in life. It is vital
  that students believe in their capacities to learn.

- *Equity.* Equity means strategically providing a range of resources and
  experiences to students in different ways so that the learning potential
  of all students is maximized. Conversations foster equity by getting
  students to interact with students of different backgrounds, language
  proficiencies, and abilities. As the teacher, you can and should provide
  varying supports before, during, and after the conversations, but the
  conversations and the students will do most of the work. We become
  more like those with whom we interact. As students interact with others,
  they are always pushed, cognitively and linguistically, to understand
  what others say and how they feel. This moves *everyone* forward. Even if
  Ana is more English proficient than David, she benefits from striving to
  communicate her thoughts with him and from learning more about how
  he, from his different background, thinks and feels.

- *Formative assessment.* Conversations offer excellent windows into what students know and can do, as well as who they are and who they want to be. This allows you to make appropriate adjustments and additions to future lessons in order to improve their learning. The downside, of course, is that you can't take all of their conversations home every night and "grade them." (If you can do this, please contact me. I have some questions for you.) But we can observe a few conversations each day and learn a lot about students' learning.

Preparing for Conversations

In a sense, this whole book is meant to help you prepare yourself, your lessons, and your students for having effective conversations. But here I want to highlight that, in addition to the very necessary conversation skills that follow, students need to have enough content in their heads to talk about, along with enough language to express that content. The content and language don't need to be perfect, by any means, but there is a certain "amount" that both participants need to have for the conversation to work.

I mention this because it isn't fair to tell students to have a rich conversation about something they know little about, or to tell two beginning English learners to converse in English about a difficult text that was just read aloud to them. What would you think if I asked you to have a conversation with a friend focused on the prompt, *Evaluate Kant's proposed solution to the question* How are a priori synthetic judgments possible? *as described in his* Critique of Pure Reason? Even if you wanted to answer this (anyone, anyone?), you would likely need to dig into the text to gain some information to work with. (And it would take even longer if the text were in German.)

You may need to make some changes in what and how you teach to make sure your students have sufficient levels of content and skills to converse about a topic. If you have been teaching to help students do well on tests, their test-based knowledge, and how it is organized in their brains, is often different from the knowledge needed for conversations. For example, if you are teaching the key facts, people, and events of the Civil War, students might have sequential or mnemonic systems for remembering them. But if students need to converse about whether slavery or states' rights was a more influential cause of the war, they will need to learn and organize their ideas differently. Instead of putting events in cause-effect sequence, for example, they need to stack up evidence for each side of the argument and decide which is heavier (see Chapter 3).

So, in a nutshell, make sure that students have enough content and language to build up ideas in extended conversation. They are not just answering basic questions or conducting an interview. Help students learn facts, evidence, and concepts that they can use in their conversations. You will often find that students walk away from those conversations with learning that is more solidified than it was when they entered.

Core Academic Conversation Skills

Good conversations have a lot going on in them. Many cognitive, verbal, and nonverbal skills need to be used during and between turns. This section introduces you to the core skills that should be in most, if not all, of your students' conversations, regardless of content area. The five core skills, shown in Figure 1.1 are (1) building ideas, (2) posing initial ideas, (3) clarifying, (4) supporting with evidence, and (5) evaluating evidence in argument-based situations.

If you just glanced at Figure 1.1, and if you know the focal skills outlined in the first *Academic Conversations* book, you have likely noticed that the skills here are slightly different and that the visual organizer is different. In my work in classrooms and in my analyses of conversations over the years, I saw that building up an idea was more important, more needed, and more challenging than I had previously thought. It's so important, in fact, that it gets its own chapter in this book. And I noticed in many conversations that students were elaborating, paraphrasing, and synthesizing in order to clarify ideas, so I put these strategies (and several others that I noticed) under the skill of clarifying. Since the first book, I have also observed the power of evaluating and comparing in argumentation-based conversations, which I have put in place of the skill called building on or challenging ideas. And, finally, I added the skill of posing buildable ideas to highlight the importance of coming up with and choosing an initial idea that is meaty and valuable for learning.

Each of these skills is actually a two-way skill. Students need to be able both to prompt partners to build, pose, clarify, support, and evaluate and compare at the right times in a conversation, and to use those skills effectively themselves when prompted by others.

A typical sequence of skills used in a conversation might be as follows. Posing one or more initial ideas tends to come first, for obvious reasons. Then students use clarifying and supporting to build up the idea. If it's an argument, students build up the competing ideas and then use the skill of evaluating and comparing evidence to decide which side is stronger, better, or heavier.

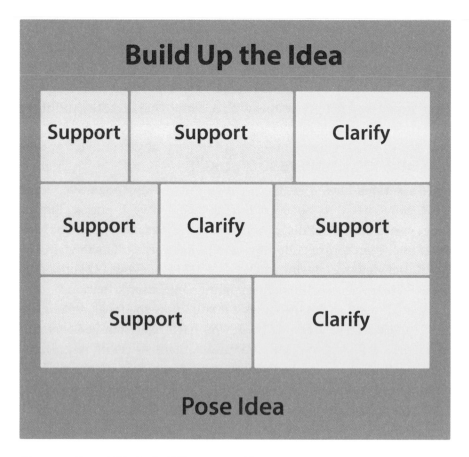

Figure 1.1 Core skills for building up one idea

Skill 1—Building an Idea

The overarching skill, as you can see in Figure 1.1, is building up one or more ideas. Every conversation should build up at least one idea, and students need to manage this process. They can't just use the skills three times each and hope an idea gets built. It's a little like a person who manages the construction of a real building. A lot of skilled workers are doing their jobs, but someone needs to have a big picture so that the workers don't forget to put in the support beams or the plumbing.

Many students and adults think of conversations as free-association time or brainstorm sessions, in which participants either connect randomly to previous ideas or share randomly ("popcorn out") a variety of different ideas. But without doing the work of focusing on and building up an idea, these kinds of talk will not become academic conversations.

I have seen many conversations in which students are using the conversation skills in Figure 1.1 but don't manage or organize these skills for building up ideas. They don't realize that building ideas is what the other conversation skills are for. Rather, students think that the skills are just a few more things that they need to show the teacher in order to check off the list or rubric to get points. For example, if tomorrow you ask your students to support ideas with evidence, how many will think, "Doing this will help us build up an important idea," and how many will think, "This is yet another thing we gotta do for school?" We must change the mindset that learning consists of memorizing disconnected piles of information, and conversations are great opportunities to practice what I call a *building ideas mindset*.

One of the first steps toward this mindset is defining what it means to build up an idea. To build an idea, people use three main skills: (1) posing a relevant and buildable idea, (2) clarifying terms used to describe it, and (3) supporting it with evidence, examples, and explanations. Here is an example from fifth-grade history, prompted by the question, *Do you think Lewis and Clark were a good team to lead their expedition?* Look for idea-building in the conversation.

(1) A: I think they were a good team.

(2) B: Why?

(3) A: Cuz Clark, he knows about nature and can make the boat. Lewis looks like the doctor and/

(4) B: And Clark knows everything about plants.

(5) A: How does that help?

(6) B: They would have to eat some plants and not eat the poison ones. Maybe they had to find them for medicine, too. I don't know.

(7) A: And the other guy knows about other things.

(8) B: You mean Lewis?

(9) A: Yeah.

(10) B: What other things?

(11) A: Maybe like he can read maps.

(12) B: Did they have maps?

(13) A: I don't think the whole trip, but maybe/

(14) B: /The first part of it, yeah.

(15) A: So maybe he knows how to make maps.

(16) B: I agree. So I think they were a good team, too.

Did you see how they co-built up an idea (Lewis and Clark were a good team) that was not in either of their minds at the start of the conversation? This is the power, beauty, and messiness of conversations. They often go in directions that the partners (or you) didn't plan on going. Granted, this direction can also take them out on rabbit trails to nowhere at times, but at other times—and this book is trying to increase these times—students can co-build valuable and lasting ideas. Chapter 2 focuses more on the skill of building ideas and describes activities for helping students to value idea-building and get better at it.

Skill 2—Pose Buildable Ideas

Students need to start by posing at least one relevant and buildable idea. If they start with just a fact, such as "George Washington was the first president," there isn't much to build on. But if the idea is abstract, complex, or an opinion, it is likely more buildable (e.g., "Thomas Jefferson accused George Washington of treason"). The building of such ideas helps students think and learn as they work with others to clarify and support them. As you already know, students pose great ideas all the time. Then again, as you also know, students can pose a wide range of non-buildable ideas. These non-buildable ideas are often in the form of facts, jokes, short answers, and irrelevant thoughts. One of our goals, then, is to develop students' abilities to filter out the non-buildable ideas and to choose and use the most buildable ones.

In the case of an argument, students need to pose two or more competing ideas and build up both of them. I recommend building one after the other, if possible, but students can add and subtract from either idea at any time.

Skill 3—Clarify

One of two main skills needed for building an idea is *clarifying*. Clarifying means getting everyone on the same-ish page with respect to what an idea, or a word, or anything else means. You want to hear questions such as "What does that mean for us?" "How do you define freedom?" "Can you repeat that?" and other questions that bring up needed information. Clarifying is a skill that depends on other key skills, such as defining, questioning, elaborating, synthesizing, paraphrasing, and negotiating the meaning of words and expressions. Elaboration, for example, helps partners get a more expanded picture of an idea and its details. Paraphrasing helps clarify what your partner just said by listing the highlights and relevant parts needed to move on. And synthesizing helps students gather up and clarify the key thoughts and pieces used in the conversation thus far.

I often see lessons and curriculums that prompt students to ask their own questions. But even though students do ask a wide range of questions when prompted, often I sense that the questions aren't authentic and that students are just asking questions because they are asked to ask them. Or I hear some small-scale, disconnected question that pops into a student's brain, such as "What did he feed his dog?" Questions, particularly in a conversation (and in most situations), need to be used to build up an idea, and students must learn to prune away the ones that don't do this.

Skill 4—Support

Supporting ideas means using examples, evidence, and reasoning to logically back up and strengthen an idea. This is an essential skill for effective conversations in school, in the workplace, and in life. In science, students must use lab data to support their written conclusions. In history, students need to use primary source evidence to support an opinion that something caused something else to happen. In math, they need to refer to mathematical principles to support a claim or a generalization about a pattern they noticed. In language arts, students must use evidence of character actions and words in a novel to support a theme.

A major challenge that many students face is gauging the strength of evidence. For too many students, searching for examples of evidence means selecting the first three that come along, even if they are on the first page of the novel. In students' minds, evidences are answers or blanks to fill in. We must instead cultivate the mindset of seeking to build up an idea as much and as well as possible. This requires finding the highest-quality evidence, even if it means extra reading. We will work on how students can determine the strength of evidence in more depth in Chapter 3.

Skill 5— Evaluate, Compare, and Choose One Idea over Others

This is the primary skill needed for deciding which idea is strongest when there are two or more competing ideas in an argument or a decision. This is shown in Figure 1.2. Academic argumentation is not only engaging: it is essential for learning. Students need to learn how to objectively and logically decide which idea or side is the best in a given situation. This should happen in typical arguments, such as *Should we let students use cell phones in school?* as well as deciding between two choices, such as *Should I go to the party or study for my math test?* In most arguments and decisions in school and in life, people should build up both sides of the issue (or all sides, if there are more than two) and then see which side weighs more, evidence-wise.

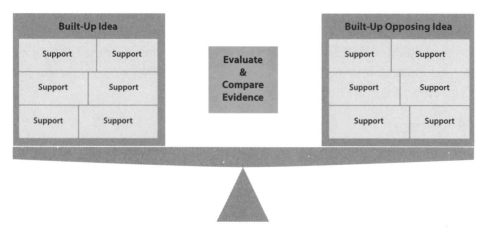

Figure 1.2 Visual model for collaborative arguments

To evaluate and compare evidence in academic settings, students need to learn to use criteria. Criteria are categories or filters that allow a person to assign value to evidence. Some criteria are easier to evaluate, such as health risks, financial costs of two different programs, or statistical data resulting from different studies on the topic. Other criteria are fuzzier and more likely to vary in students' minds, such as the ethics of each side, biases, psychological effects, and short-term benefits versus long-term benefits. Of course, a person's values and feelings about a certain issue can have a lot of influence on the person's use of criteria.

Let's look at an example. In the following conversation, two seventh graders are deciding whether the Black Death was good or bad, overall, for the development of Europe. There are two ideas to build up and then evaluate.

(1)	A:	So let's do the good side first.
(2)	B:	Something about a Ren-. . . , Renaissance.
(3)	A:	I forgot what that was.
(4)	B:	It was when they, like, did a lot more art and science, I think. Remember the pictures of all those paintings?
(5)	A:	Yeah, I guess that was all good. Here it says that serfdom stopped.
(6)	B:	What was that?
(7)	A:	Serfs were like poor workers, like slaves. They just worked on land for the owners, and I think like they got a part of it to eat. Something like that.
(8)	B:	So it's good that it stopped, and they got to work for money.
(9)	A:	Yeah. What about the bad.
(10)	B:	Well, lots of people died.
(11)	A:	That's really bad. And here it says that some people stopped believing in God.
(12)	B:	Why?

These students did an acceptable amount of evaluating, compared with the norm of very little in most classroom conversations. Often, students build up one or more sides partway, but then they are cut off by time or they are too tired to do the extra thinking it takes to evaluate at the end of a conversation. In this conversation, they didn't mention criteria, per se, which I would have liked to hear, but they did consider the criterion of number of deaths to be heavier than the other criteria of reduced serfdom and the Renaissance.

Also, notice that these students didn't start with their opinions. Often, when people start a conversation with an opinion, they feel they need to back it up, stick to it, and in many cases, win the argument at all costs. Yet, when they start with building up both sides, reserving their opinions (or at least keeping them in the back of their minds) until later, they allow themselves to become more informed about each side, so that they can then make a more objective decision near the end of the conversation. And they don't turn others off with over-competitiveness during the entire conversation. Encourage students to reserve their biases and opinions as much as possible until they have built up each side.

Notice in Figure 1.2 that this skill also supports the central skill of building ideas. This is because objectively evaluating and choosing one idea over another pushes the students to build up both ideas even more. If you don't have much competition, you don't tend to work as hard on building up a single idea.

Reinforcing the Five Skills with Gestures

An effective strategy for helping students to remember and use these skills is teaching them hand gestures for each. Students can use these during conversations or, more commonly, just refer to them in their minds as they talk.

- For the skill of building ideas, they put one hand on top of the other repeatedly, like piling up bricks.
- For posing ideas, students lay one hand out forward, with the palm up.
- For clarifying ideas, they put their hands together in front of their eyes, palms out, and then spread their hands and fingers out.
- For supporting ideas, they do the gesture for posing, and then bring the fingers and thumb of the other hand up underneath it to support it, like a table with five legs. I sometimes show them what happens if only one finger tries to support the idea (it wobbles and falls).
- And for evaluating, comparing, and choosing, they put their arms out to their sides, palms up, and move them up and down like a balance scale.

Additional Conversation Skills to Develop

The five core skills are vital, but additional skills bulk up the learning power of conversations. These include constructive listening, focused speaking, critical and creative thinking, using content, mental multitasking, and using nonverbal cues.

Constructive Listening

Constructive listening means working hard to understand what the other is saying, being aware of the conversation as a whole, being aware of what is not said, keeping track of ideas, and interpreting a speaker's tone and body language. Listening is a lot of mental work, especially when, in pairs, you have to listen to every one of your partner's turns in a conversation. The more that we can develop student habits of listening well to build ideas, the better. If a student listens to each turn without trying to build with their partner, then you often end up with a "popcorn" conversation with little substance. So, we must model and scaffold students' abilities to listen for clarification (and the need to clarify), for support (and the need to support), and for evaluation of evidence (and the need to evaluate). You will see a variety of activities in this book that help students improve their constructive listening in conversation.

Focused Speaking

Focused speaking means using language and other means of communication to get the key messages across to partners in each turn. It means speaking loudly enough, with clear pronunciation, and it often includes referring to common ideas that partners have learned in order to build from common understanding. Focused speaking is usually supported by gestures, facial expressions, emphasis on certain words and phrases, and even visuals. It does not require students to use perfect grammar or perfect vocabulary.

Focused speaking also means saying enough in each turn. As you have likely noticed, many students say too little when they answer questions and share their ideas. Some students know they should say more, but they are unmotivated by the task. Many students simply just don't realize that they should say more to be clearer. One of your roles, and one of the roles of fellow students in the class, is to model and push others to say more in conversational turns. Encourage students to say more than they think they need to say, especially the students who need extra practice articulating their ideas.

One way to build up the habit of saying enough is with more structured activities in which listeners purposefully wait for talkers to fill in the time with talk about the topic. For example, in the Transition Improvisation (Chapter 3) and Stronger and Clearer Each Time (Chapter 2) activities, there are structured times for one student to talk while the other listens. When one student says, "Zoos are bad for animals," and suddenly stops before her time is up, the listener should wait in silence for her to say more. If the talker doesn't keep talking, the listener can do one of three things: (1) ask for clarification (*What do you mean by* bad?), (2) ask for support (*What are examples of zoos being bad for animals?*), or (3) provide a seedling idea that the talker can put into her own words (*What about the animals not getting exercise?*).

Critical and Creative Thinking

Students already use critical and creative thinking skills for thinking about the world, their place in it, and how to solve life's problems. Many students already analyze and compare images, evaluate the quality of TV shows, persuade parents to let them go out, interpret the actions or words of friends, empathize with a sibling, apply what they learned from the Internet to win a video game, and so on. Our students need to transfer and extend the thinking skills they already use outside of school to the learning of academic concepts inside school. It is our job as teachers to create, model, and support experiences in which students can successfully do this in the academic arena. Table 1.1 lists various thinking skills in four content areas.

CONTENT AREA	THINKING SKILLS
SCIENCE	Observe and analyze: Focus on the phenomena you are observing, taking different perspectives, and generating possible problems
	Hypothesize: Make interpretations and predictions about the causes and effects of proposed solutions and explanations
	Experiment: Compare treatments, interpret the data, and analyze the possible influence of extraneous variables
	Reflect: Evaluate the strength of the data and synthesize them into a conclusion
	Communicate: Prepare insights and conclusions in a clear and strong way to others
	Interpret: Understand new vocabulary and abstract meanings of familiar terms that are used to describe science concepts

Table 1.1 Commonly used thinking skills in science, social studies, history, and language arts

CONTENT AREA	THINKING SKILLS
SOCIAL STUDIES AND HISTORY	Analyze: Break down and look closely at political, social, and historical processes; gather evidence by looking at documents and other physical records
	Hypothesize: Speculate on what happened, why, and what people were thinking at the time
	Interpret: See and explain inconsistencies or discrepancies of evidence with current theories and accepted ideas; understand how biased ideas influence the writings of history
	Synthesize: Combine ideas and interpretations from other observers of history and social studies
	Identify causes and effects: Determine the relations of historical and present events
	Empathize: Feel what others felt, from those who lived centuries ago to those across the street (or ocean) today; strive to filter out narcissistic and present-biased views of the world
	Compare: Find similarities in political systems, cultures, ideas, events, and perspectives
LANGUAGE ARTS	Analyze: Examine literature for key elements and devices
	Compare: Find similarities between characters, events in stories, and literary works
	Identify and infer causes and effects: Infer causal relationships between events and character changes
	Empathize: Find understanding with characters and authors
	Synthesize: Examine literary works and genres to come up with key ideas
	Interpret: Decipher literary devices, themes, and figurative language
	Evaluate: Assess the quality of a written text and the author's techniques
	Communicate: Express clearly one's own thoughts and feelings to others

Table 1.1 (continued) Commonly used thinking skills in science, social studies, history, and language arts

Notice the thinking skills used in the following conversation from fifth grade, after students had read "Inside Out," a story in Francisco Jimenez's *The Circuit* (1997). The teacher had asked them to share their ideas for themes in the story. They had also talked about symbols and how they can emphasize themes.

---

(1) A: I thought it was being patient, you know, waiting. And the symbol for it was the caterpillar.

(2) B: Can you explain that?

(3) A: The caterpillar just crawls around. And he's trapped in the jar. Francisco was kinda trapped, too. He had to wait to learn English to talk to people and be happy.

(4) B: So you think that Francisco was like that caterpillar cuz he waited? I can add to that. He didn't quit school. And he didn't yell at the teacher, like when she took his drawing away.

(5) A: Yeah, and when he got the ribbon and that guy liked the drawing. That made him happy, like a butterfly. *(Pause).* What's your theme?

(6) B: It's kinda like yours. I think it's to try hard.

(7) A: Why?

(8) B: Francisco was scared like when he looked at the jar, and when other kids looked at him. But he stayed and tried hard to learn English.

(9) A: And another thing for try hard was he looked at the books to learn. He tried to learn, but he didn't read English.

(10) B: Yeah. And he made art. He tried to make beautiful pictures and won the prize. But the caterpillar? Maybe the caterpillar tries hard to make his cocoon thing.

(11) A: And that helps him turn into a butterfly.

Also notice that there isn't a lot of what is typically considered academic language in this conversation. This is OK. These two students are pushing themselves to think abstractly, interpret complex text, use evidence, and apply ideas to new contexts. These skills, for the moment, are more important than using academic vocabulary and correct grammar in their sentences. In many cases, when teachers impose language frames on students, conversation is stilted and often stalls. Students need the freedom to engage with each other and get excited about the new ideas that emerge in whatever language(s) they prefer to use. Academic language will develop over time as students immerse themselves in academic texts and conversations based on them.

Using Content

What you also noticed in the previous conversation was a useful understanding of content. In order to co-build ideas with others, students need to know how ideas are built up and used in a discipline, and they need to have enough facts, concepts, and discipline-specific skills. This content comes from previous conversations, reading, writing, watching, and other learning activities. We must cultivate in students the sense that the content and skills they are learning will be *used,* and that they will have some agency and control over how they will be used.

The content should be as accurate and true as possible. One of the maxims of effective conversation is that people must not purposefully say false things (Grice 1975). We must keep reminding students to refer to texts, to question biases, to think critically, and to pursue truth as they converse with others. Notice the reference to a content principle (using a mathematical law) in the next conversation from a high school algebra class.

---

(1)   A: I think we might need to use the quadratic equation.

(2)   B: Ugh. Why don't we just change the problem so we can factor it.

(3)   A: What?

(4)   B: We just change this number here to a 4.

(5)   A: We can't change the problem.

(6)   B: Why not?

(7)   A: You just can't. It's like a math law or something like that.

Mental Multitasking

Like a construction crew that works together to create a large building, the brain tends to do many things simultaneously in a conversation. To decide what to say next, we listen to and process what our partners is saying. We think about what new ideas the partner is adding to the mix and how valuable they are. We consider how clear the partner is and whether to clarify something he or she has said. We think about the details, connections, or evidence that we might add to what the partner is saying. We prune away irrelevant or inappropriate thoughts. We reflect on how we might be as clear as possible in our next turn. We might think about how to paraphrase what the partner said to see whether we understood, or we might respectfully challenge something the partner said. All of these types of moves, or turns, should be focused on building one or more ideas. If they don't have the purpose of building, they are likely not worth precious class time or conversational energy.

Students also need to know how long, more or less, the conversation should be. Most of the time, student conversations end way too soon, before they have built up their idea enough. Some teachers have students use cards to extend conversations (see Idea-Building Cards in Chapter 2 and Silent Support Cards in Chapter 6). Some teachers use third "observer-coaches" to take notes on the building process (see Chapters 2 and 6). Always watch to make sure students are not just trying to make you happy or to get points by saying things simply to use up their cards (e.g., asking questions, clarifying, supporting). Students should always be thinking, "How can we keep building up this idea to make it as clear and strong as possible?" There are ideas for cultivating this mindset in students in Chapter 6.

Using Nonverbal Cues

A large amount of face-to-face communication is nonverbal. Students need to use appropriate nonverbal cues, such as eye contact, head nods, posture, and hand gestures to both listen and speak effectively with partners. A lot of the fluency in using these cues develops from immersion in conversations with a wide range of others. Yes, you should model these cues and point them out as you observe students' conversations, but you should also give students plenty of opportunities to practice using and interpreting them with others in real conversations.

Improving Conversation Prompts

A common question that often emerges in this work is how to improve conversation prompts. The prompt can make a big difference in the quality of conversations. As most teachers know all too well, you can't just lift questions out of the published curriculum and use them as prompts. They might provide some initial ideas, but you have to make adjustments because you know your students: what they know, what they need to know, what interests them, and what they need to work on with respect to conversation skills.

Here are several features of effective conversation prompts that you can use to improve prompts in your setting.

1. **The prompt has an engaging purpose** that requires building one or more ideas in support of the objectives of the lesson and unit. For example, you can't just say, *Talk about this text for several minutes* and expect students to put much effort into conversing. Students need to know why they are talking to others so that they can muster up the energy that it takes to converse effectively. A prompt should require reshaping, choosing, or doing something with ideas. Here are some verbs that you might use: *agree on, create, clarify, argue, decide, rank, prioritize, come up with, solve, evaluate, combine, compare, choose, fortify, build, weigh,* and *transform.*

2. **The prompt creates a need to talk** by setting up a requirement for the students to share information. The conversation is usually a part of a larger task, and students are better able to do the task by thinking with others than by themselves. The prompt thus leverages the different knowledges, perspectives, and skills that students bring and can share with one another. Students, after reading the prompt, should think, "In order to ____, I need to have a good conversation with one or more peers." (You can also think about what might engage *you* enough to converse if you were a typical student.)

3. **The prompt contains clear expectations and directions** that tell students what to do to have effective conversations. This often makes your prompts longer than just a question. You might include which skills to use, the final "product" of the conversation, and any other specifics that your students need to do to build up ideas.

The most effective prompts are not created at the last minute. Curriculum materials often try to provide conversation prompts, but they tend to be weak or just another question used to test comprehension of a text. A good prompt comes from your teacher knowledge of who your students are, what they need to work on, and what they are interested in. Most published curriculums don't provide strong enough conversation prompts because, unlike you, they're unable to tailor the prompts to your students' background knowledge.

In Table 1.2, notice that the prompts on the left are missing one or more of the three features of effective conversation prompts. Our first draft prompts often look like the ones on the left. The goal is to strengthen them as effectively and as often as possible with the features.

LESS EFFECTIVE AND INCOMPLETE PROMPTS	EFFECTIVE PROMPTS
In your conversations, talk about themes that came up in the story.	What do you think readers are supposed to learn from the main character in this book? How are we supposed to be better people? Use parts of the story to support your ideas.
Describe the polar bear to each other.	How do adaptations help the polar bear survive in its habitat? I would like to hear you use sentences like this one: "If a polar bear didn't . . . , it probably wouldn't survive because . . ."
Discuss this math problem and how to solve it.	Work with your partner to come up with two ways to solve this problem. Ask each other "why" questions as you talk to explain why you are choosing to do certain things.
In your conversation, summarize what you read about your famous historical person.	With your partner, come up with a description of how to be a famous person in history. I want to be famous. What do I need to do? What do I need to say? What kind of personality do I need? Use the stories you read. And don't forget to ask your partner to clarify, if he or she doesn't say enough.

Table 1.2 From less effective to more effective prompts

As you can see by the examples on the right, effective prompts (a) allow students to share what they know and to shape ideas with partners, without being too open; and (b) are more work to create. But you will quickly see positive results as you work on beefing up your prompts in these ways.

Here are some additional examples of prompts:

- Decide which theme in the story is most relevant for fourth graders today. Choose the strongest two themes, build them up with evidence from the story, and then decide which one is more needed for improving your world.
- Agree on how you would measure the speed of sound. Pose several possible experiments, evaluate the benefits and potential accuracy of each, and then decide on one that you will describe in detail.
- Discuss how to solve this problem two different ways, compare them, and argue for the use of one of them in future problems that are similar. Use mathematical reasoning to justify your procedures along the way.
- Rank the qualities of a good friend. Make an initial list of qualities and

then decide which one is the most important, the next most important, and so on. Be able to explain why one quality is more important than the next one on your priority list. Also discuss if you or your partner need to work on any of the qualities to be a better friend to others.

- For our museum project, work with a partner to decide on the clearest way to describe the importance of your artifact and what it tells us about people in that time period. Discuss what makes the artifact important and how archaeologists used it to learn about the people who created it. Then come up with a final display and written description.

When students think that a conversation is just another pair-share to say a short answer and listen to a partner's answer, conversation doesn't happen. We want them to be excited by the prompt and by the chance to think together with others about it. Students need to see conversations as vital stages in the idea-building process.

Strategies for Using Standards to Come Up with Effective Conversation Prompts

Learning standards, in general, are not written with conversations in mind. Yes, there are often some oral, listening, and conversation-esque standards in there, but the overall structure is a long list of facts, concepts, and skills to learn. Published curriculums covering these standards then tend to frame their designs and approaches in list-like fashion. We, therefore, need to be creative in crafting lessons and prompts that help students focus on posing, choosing, and building up robust ideas.

Here are three strategies for using standards to generate effective prompts, which are focused on what I call *conversation-worthy* ideas. You can look at most reading, writing, and content standards to get ideas for prompts. The first column in each chart includes the standard, and the second column has a draft prompt that asks students to build up one or more ideas based on that standard. I try to include the other two main features of prompts (need to talk, clear expectations and directions), but these two will tend to differ, depending on the students and curriculum.

1. Analyze the standards for concepts that (a) contain multiple parts, components, sub-ideas, evidence, connections, or examples; (b) require multiple sentences to describe them; (c) will have differing descriptions

across students; and (d) can keep building up in student minds beyond this unit and into the future. Of course, some standards require less creativity than others in terms of finding and using them to come up with conversation-worthy ideas. See Table 1.3 for examples.

STANDARDS	DRAFT PROMPTS THAT CALL FOR THE BUILDING OF CONVERSATION-WORTHY IDEAS
Write opinion pieces on topics or texts, supporting a point of view with reasons. (CCSS.ELA-LITERACY.W.3.1)	Work with a partner to build up your opinion on whether third graders should be allowed to watch TV. You should ask each other to come up with good reasons and to describe them as clearly as possible. Use examples to strengthen your idea.
Construct and present arguments using evidence to support the claim that gravitational interactions are attractive and depend on the masses of interacting objects. (NGSS-MS-PS2.4)	Look at the data table that shows how much a person and a truck weigh on different planetary bodies (Earth, moon, sun, meteor), and use this as evidence for the law that the attraction between two objects depends on the masses. Also talk about why the same person weighs less at the top of Mount Everest than at sea level.
Recognize angle measure as additive. When an angle is decomposed into nonoverlapping parts, the angle measure of the whole is the sum of the angle measures of the parts. Solve addition and subtraction problems to find unknown angles on a diagram in real-world and mathematical problems , e.g., by using an equation with a symbol for the unknown angle measure. (CCSS.MATH.CONTENT.4.MD.C.7)	Collaborate with a partner to solve the following problem (*A road crossed a train track at an angle of 35 degrees . . .*). Come up with an equation that includes a symbol for the unknown angle, and be able to explain how to solve this problem, and others like it, to others. Then converse to co-create a word problem in which the solver has to find one or more unknown angles on a diagram.
Students will examine the reasons for economic prosperity during the 1920s. Students will examine the underlying weaknesses of the economy that led to the stock market crash of 1929 and the Great Depression. (New York State Social Studies 2015, Framework.11.7c)	Converse with a partner to build up the idea of whether the Great Depression could have been avoided. Talk about the top reasons for the prosperity of the 1920s and the main weaknesses that led to the stock market crash of 1929 and the Great Depression. Hindsight is twenty-twenty, but what might you have done as president during the 1920s to prevent the Depression?

Table 1.3 Using standards to craft conversation-worthy prompts

2. Look for arguments, controversial issues, and decisions to be made. When students need to build up both sides before choosing one, they do double the building. Then, they evaluate evidence on each side to choose which one is stronger. (Chapter 3 covers these types of conversations in detail.) Here are some examples of what to look for in the standards (see Table 1.4).

STANDARDS	DRAFT PROMPTS THAT CALL FOR THE BUILDING OF CONVERSATION-WORTHY IDEAS
Analyze how two or more authors writing about the same topic shape their presentations of key information by emphasizing different evidence or advancing different interpretations of facts. (CCSS.ELA-LITERACY.RI.7.9)	After reading two articles that take opposing sides on the same issue, discuss how the authors built up their claims, and decide which is stronger.
Construct an argument that plants and animals have internal and external structures that function to support survival, growth, behavior, and reproduction. (NGSS-4-LS1-1)	Talk with your partner to clarify and support the idea that plants and animals have internal and external traits that help them survive. Also build up the opposite side that traits are random or purposeless.
Decide whether two quantities are in a proportional relationship, e.g., by testing for equivalent ratios in a table or graphing on a coordinate plane and observing whether the graph is a straight line through the origin. (CCSS.MATH.CONTENT.7.RP.A.2.A)	Work with a partner to decide whether two quantities are in a certain proportional relationship. Justify your decision with at least two methods.
Learn about the explorers' European origins, motives, journeys, and the enduring historical significance of their voyages to the Americas. Learn important factors that contributed to the age of exploration. (*California History-Social Science Framework*, Fifth Grade California State Board of Education 2017)	Work with a partner to decide what you think were the two strongest factors that motivated Europeans to explore; build up both with evidence and then decide which was the strongest.

Table 1.4 Using standards to craft argumentation-based conversation prompts

3. Look for language in the standards that describes academic thinking skills, usually, entailing larger concepts or ideas. The juiciest skills to look for are identifying causes and effects, interpreting, making inferences, evaluating, synthesizing, empathizing, comparing, and solving.

Remember that most humans don't want to do this mental work without some good motivation or purpose for doing it. Just telling two students to compare the two stories in order to work on their comparing skills won't be as effective as having an engaging purpose for comparing them. Table 1.5 has some examples of using standards to generate initial drafts of conversation prompts. The terms describing thinking skills are in green.

STANDARDS	DRAFT PROMPTS THAT CALL FOR THE BUILDING OF CONVERSATION-WORTHY IDEAS
Evaluate a speaker's point of view, reasoning, and use of evidence and rhetoric, identifying any fallacious reasoning or exaggerated or distorted evidence. (CCSS.ELA-LITERACY.SL.9-10.3)	After listening to William Faulkner's Nobel Prize acceptance speech, converse to come up with a solid idea for what he wanted listeners to think and do in response. What does it mean to "create out of the materials of the human spirit something which did not exist before?" Evaluate how well he supports his ideas and whether this support is strong or not—and why.
Analyze and interpret data on the distribution of fossils and rocks, continental shapes, and seafloor structures to provide evidence of the past plate motions. (NGSS-MS-ESS2-3)	Collaborate to come up with a solid idea that describes past plate motions using your interpretations of the data on the distribution of fossil shapes and rocks, shapes of the continents, and seafloor geology. Talk about how your idea might be used to predict what the Earth will look like in a million years.
Solve systems of linear equations exactly and approximately (e.g., with graphs), focusing on pairs of linear equations in two variables. (CCSS.MATH.CONTENT.HSA.REI.C.6)	Collaborate to solve the following problem. *(Students at a school started two businesses. The first business started in January and sold . . .)* Start by approximating the answer by graphing. Then, solve the problem to get the exact answer. Both of you should prepare to justify each step that you use. Finally, come up with an idea that uses this problem as an example *(To solve problems like these, we . . .).*
Understands various forms of government and their effects on the lives of people in the past or present (e.g., compares and contrasts the effects of feudalism on the lives of people in medieval Europe and Japan). (WashingtonState.G7.1.2.3.)	Converse to come up with the most important similarities and differences between ways in which feudalism in medieval Europe and Japan affected people's lives. Co-compose a letter from a person who has lived in both systems arguing, his or her preference for one over the other.

Table 1.5 Using standards to craft conversation prompts based on academic thinking skills

Did you notice how these prompts ask students to build up potentially engaging ideas? As you can see, I used a lot of the language of the standards in the right-hand column, but I added more interesting purposes for talking to make the idea-building more engaging for students. And even though the ideas on the right could be used as prompts as they now stand, in real life I would beef them up even more with the three features of effective conversation prompts.

Conclusion

Conversations tend to be diverse, incomplete, and messy. They are all different, and they are a lot of mental work. It would be much easier for us and for our students to simply memorize definitions, short answers, facts, and grammar rules than to build complex ideas in constructive conversations. Despite the challenges, though, we know that having academic conversations is necessary for students' academic development (Baker, Jensen, and Kolb 2002). By valuing conversations between people, we are shaping our students' views of how we learn and live. When they see the value of learning by talking with others, building up ideas, and making decisions, their views of learning are amplified. This process, however, does take a lot of work and practice, and the remaining chapters of this book are here to help.

Chapter 2

Building Ideas

It's time to let all students build up big cities of ideas in their minds.

If a student said to you, "I don't want to live forever" or "The energy in gasoline started with the sun," would either statement be enough to convince you of their learning of the concepts? I, for one, would want to hear more. But, is one sentence (or even just one word) enough for fellow students? Unfortunately, and usually, yes. That's one of the big problems hindering good conversations in school. If partners listen to short statements and just say "I agree" or "Yeah," because they don't see a need to build up an idea, then the conversation withers.

But it's not our students' fault. Schooling has trained them to cut their thinking short and to provide minimal answers because time—class time and test time—is so limited. Nor have long lists of standards to cover encouraged curriculum writers or teachers to get students to do the hard work of connecting, reinforcing, and building up meaty ideas. It's easier to have students just pile up discrete pieces. High-stakes end-of-year assessments further encourage this piling with their random texts and multiple-choice questions.

In this book, the term *idea* has a broad definition. An idea can be a concept, claim, hypothesis, theme, solution method, process, pattern, conclusion, explanation, description, interpretation, or an answer to a big question. It's anything academically valuable that needs multiple sentences to describe, usually including clarifying and supporting with evidence and details.

Students need to see that an idea is not just one more little thing to memorize. Ideas can change and evolve over time. They can be sculpted, strengthened, and pruned, and they can live and thrive beyond school walls and beyond graduation.

They can be composed of smaller ideas, and they can be parts of larger ideas. They can be—and often need to be—communicated to different people in different ways. For example, a fifth-grade student begins to build the idea that the history textbook is a secondary source based on primary sources, many of which are biased. She begins to ask questions about the accuracy of the textbook and about the motivations of the authors of primary sources. These answers, and further questions that usually clarify or support the idea, help her to start building up this idea, which will likely last throughout her life, such as when she applies it to news articles.

When it comes to students appreciating idea-building, it's a bit of a chicken-or-egg situation. If students don't get a lot of experiences building ideas, alone or with others, then they don't tend to value the building or the ideas. But the more they value both the ideas and the process of building them, the more they will build, and so on. Yet, in the limited "memorize and multiple choice" view of learning, students rarely see the need to do the extra cognitive work of building up ideas. So, to tell students to work together to expand, to connect, and to say more about what they are learning is a major shift in how and what they are learning.

When doing this work, a tension tends to arise between the positive engagement that comes from building up ideas and the negative disengagement that comes from the extra mental effort it takes. True, some students will always welcome this engaging work. But other students, the ones we are most concerned about, can waver in their interest and motivation. For these students, we must be highly creative, responsive, and supportive as we design instruction and assessments. We want their scales to tip toward "I'm engaged enough to put some extra effort into this," rather than "This is too much work for what I get out of it."

When a teacher or text asks a question, most students do not tend to think, "This question asks for an answer that I need to build up by clarifying and supporting it with evidence." For many, the thinking might be, "I sure hope I'm not called on, but if I am, what is the bare minimum I can say to get the teacher to move on?" Or, "What's the bare minimum I can say to get points (or other rewards)?" Now, even though you might think that I am stereotyping students or calling them lazy, I'm not. All students want to learn, and what we have done to them through mile-wide, inch-deep, disconnected, silent, test-focused curriculums is to blame.

Therefore, getting students to understand what building up an idea means is an enormous and exciting challenge. We need to prioritize students' idea-building habits and skills. This chapter therefore provides practical activities and strategies for developing conversation skills that are needed to build up ideas. A brief description of the skill is followed by descriptions of activities, strategies, practices, and habits that are effective for strengthening the skill. I have placed some activities that are a bit more structured directly underneath certain skills. And I put the activities in which students need to use all three skills in tandem under the first skill, building ideas.

Skill 1—Building Ideas

Building one or more ideas is the master skill that manages the other skills. In order to work together in conversation to build an idea, students need to listen, observe nonverbal cues, evaluate evidence, notice lacks of clarity, clarify, provide evidence, validate partner turns, and more. Let's say you and I are students and we are conversing. I need to listen well to you, which means that I need to listen to what you are saying to see how relevant and clear your idea is. Is it an idea worth building, or if we are already building up an idea, is what you are sharing helpful? If not, what do I say? If so, what do I say? Does something need to be clearer? Do I need to be clearer? All the while, as I am listening I'm also thinking about what I will say next, altering it based on what you are saying and what we have already said. Throughout the conversation, we both are using lots of gestures and facial expressions, thinking skills (e.g., cause-effect, empathy, analyzing, evaluating, comparing, interpreting, problem solving), and knowledge to build up our idea or ideas.

Ultimately, we want students to be so proficient at building ideas that they default to it as much as possible each time they talk to partners. We want them to think of conversations as creative working spaces that they jump into with enthusiasm because they are excited about building something that wasn't there before. At the same time, we want them to feel "academic discomfort" when an idea is only partially formed, so that they feel the need and desire to push themselves and others toward building up ideas that are as robust and as clear as possible. Yes, I know that there are a lot of wants in this paragraph, but they can happen.

Idea-Building Cards

This activity has students literally build up an idea with cards as they converse. It is an effective way to show them how the key skills work together to strengthen and support ideas, push them to do more supporting and clarifying, and help them see what might be missing. If, for example, they end up with a stack with just a few support cards, they might realize the need to share and request more evidence to support the idea. Here is the procedure.

Figure 2.1 Sample stack of Idea-Building Cards

1. Generate a prompt that allows students to build up a relevant learning idea. The prompt can come from an essential question, standard, or curriculum, but make sure that there is potential for using multiple clarify and support turns (which become cards). (See the end of Chapter 1 for additional suggestions for crafting prompts.)

2. Set up triads that have two talkers and one observer-coach. Decide which person will be the observer-coach. This student does the building. Hand out three idea cards, eight clarify cards, and eight support cards to this person. (You can also use more three-dimensional objects such as cubes and blocks to show the building.) If argumentation is involved, hand out four evaluate-and-compare cards to the observer-coach. Later on in the year you can have dyads in which each person in a pair helps to build up the idea, but begin with a dedicated observer-coach, because it takes extra thinking and energy to handle the cards and participate in the conversation at the same time.

3. Have students think about the prompt before starting their conversation. All three write down a starter idea or two on sticky notes.

4. The two talkers decide which idea is most buildable and relevant. They should agree that it is relevant to their learning and worthy of building up in a conversation. They put that sticky note on the idea card (purple) in the middle. They can set aside the other idea cards and build them up later if they want.

5. Either talker can then ask a clarify question or a support question, and the observer-coach, if possible, writes down a quick note (a few words) on a clarify (pink) or support (blue) card to remember its gist. Then the observer-coach slips the card under the idea card as a way to build up the idea. The other student clarifies or supports, and the observer-coach again jots a quick note on a new card and puts it underneath the idea card. Prompts and responses each get a card. The notes on the cards help to keep track of the evidence, examples, and clarifications. Also, it is possible that when asked to clarify, a student might respond with an example, which means using a different-colored card, and that is fine. Remind observer-coaches that if they are not sure whether they should insert pink or blue, it doesn't matter: they can choose either color because the two skills tend to overlap. As long as the response seems useful for building, either type of card is OK.

6. As talkers provide support, they should ask each other to explain (warrant) how and how well, the evidence, example, or reasoning supports the idea. These prompts could get either type of card, though I suggest clarify cards so that the support cards can be reserved for new evidence and examples that support the idea.

7. They continue to talk, and the observer-coach keeps slipping cards underneath the idea to build it up as high as possible. Remind students not to say just anything to get a card under the idea but, rather, to be thoughtful in making each of their turns as clear, strong, and useful for building up the idea as possible. It is their idea, and it may end up in their brains for a long time.

8. If it is an argument, after building up both ideas (i.e., piling up two stacks of cards), the observer-coach extracts the clarify cards and then the talkers evaluate and compare the evidences on each side. The observer-coach places evaluate-and-compare cards between the two stacks. One student might ask, "So which one is stronger?" and the observer-coach puts down an evaluate card. And the other might respond, "I think the statistics on the temperature change over the last century are the stronger because . . . "

9. In the end, all three students should be prepared to describe (synthesize) the idea or ideas that they built up, key terms they clarified, the most salient evidence, and the idea's overall importance.

Table 2.1 provides a sample conversation from a fifth-grade math classroom, prompted by *Explain how you divide one fraction by another and why you do the procedures. Use the cards.* They start with an idea card on which they write the initial idea *To divide fractions, you turn one over and multiply.* Then they insert other cards underneath the idea card.

CONVERSATION TURNS		TYPE AND COLOR OF CARD
(1)	A: To divide you gotta turn it over and, like, multiply.	Idea (Purple)
(2)	B: But why?	Clarify (Pink)
(3)	A: Cuz multiply is opposite of divide.	Clarify (Pink)
(4)	B: But why do you turn the second one over? You don't do that with add and subtract.	Clarify (Pink)
(5)	A: I don't know. Here. What does divide mean? Maybe we use easier numbers, 6 divided by 2.	Support (Blue)
(6)	B: Three. So divide is how many times the second number fits into the first one here.	Clarify (Pink)
(7)	A: Yeah. So for fractions we do that.	Support (Blue)
(8)	B: What?	Clarify (Pink)
(9)	A: We see how many times the fraction fits into the first one.	Clarify (Pink)
(10)	B: So let's divide ½ by ¼. We see how many times ¼ fits into ½, right?	Support (Blue)
(11)	A: Yeah. Two. Look at the pie pieces. It fits two times. So, if we turn the ¼ over and get 4, 4 times ½ is 2. It works.	Support (Blue)
(12)	B: We already know it works. But why?	Clarify (Pink)
(13)	A: Cuz maybe. I don't know. It just does.	No Card Here
(14)	B: Maybe cuz look. When the bottom number gets bigger, the fraction gets smaller, right? Like 1/50 is a lot smaller than ¼. So that means 50 little pieces fit into one whole, right?	Support (Blue)
(15)	A: One whole what?	Clarify (Pink)
(16)	B: Anything. An apple, a pizza, whatever. It doesn't matter. It's one whole. So you, when you turn it over and times it, that's 50 times.	Support (Blue)
(17)	A: What? So the bigger the bottom number, the smaller piece it is.	Clarify (Pink)
(18)	B: Yeah. And so, the more times it will fit into the whole thing, one. That's why you turn it over, to know how many times it'll fit into one.	Clarify (Pink)

Table 2.1 Sample math conversation using the Idea-Building Cards

Notice how the students pushed one another to build up a better understanding of division of fractions, and notice how the cards probably helped them stay on task and see how an idea is built up with clarification and justification. The idea isn't perfect, but it is evolving, and this conversation was just one step in the job of constructing it. The teacher emphasized taking the time to understand the math, not just for using fast tricks to get right answers as quickly as possible. The teacher also emphasized working with smaller "test case" examples (the 6 divided by 2, the ½ divided by ¼, etc.), which is a vital mathematical practice.

Other Uses for the Idea-Building Cards

If you end up making the Idea-Building cards, you might as well also use them to fortify conversation skills in other interaction-based activities. In some of the cases that follow, you might want to have cards that students can write on. Here are some possible uses:

- During a whole-class discussion, pause at times to have students think about what would produce a good next turn, and then they can show the possible turns (with their cards). Let's say you are discussing the key elements of ancient civilizations and their importance. A student says, "I don't think that religion was very important." You can pause and ask, "Everyone, think about what you would say next to this student and write it on either type of card." Share them with a partner and then show them to us all.
- In the Stronger and Clearer Each Time activity (later in this chapter), students in line A can hold an envelope containing ten clarify and ten support cards. After each turn, you ask both partners to pull out one or more cards corresponding to either skill used in that turn. For example, if you (A) say that we should ban drug tests on animals, then I (B) ask you for evidence, and you respond with some evidence, then we would each take a support card. The goal would be to get at least six or so cards. Remember that, at times, a question or response could be either support or clarify; if it's helpful for building, it doesn't matter which color they choose.
- When reading an expository text, the reader can put down cards (or sticky notes) in places where he or she would like to see more or better clarification or support. This allows students to get a better view of authors' abilities to build up ideas in the minds of their readers.

- In peer editing, the reader can put down cards or sticky notes in places where the author needs to clarify or support the idea. Or, the author can read her writing aloud and have the listener put down cards when he hears that something more is needed. They then talk about the notes.

Building Ideas Visual

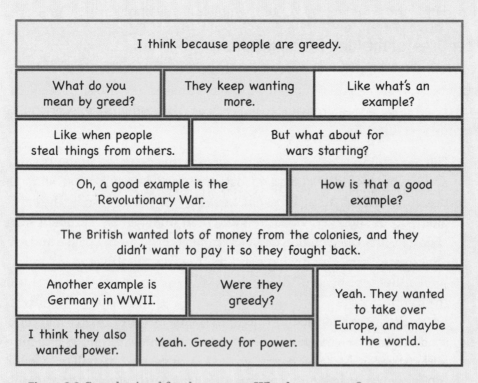

Figure 2.2 Sample visual for the prompt, *Why do wars start?*

This visual is related to the cards in the previous activity. It can be a pre-conversation organizer, a post-conversation organizer, or, with the help of an observer-coach, a during-conversation activity. It can extend well before and well beyond a conversation and can include other reading, writing, listening, and speaking activities (e.g., Socratic seminars, labs, reports). It can even be something that students fill in during an entire unit of study. In this activity, students write to keep track of the bricks used to build up their ideas. They can draw their own "buildings" or use a form like the one in Appendix A. This visual is mainly used before, after, or during a break in the conversation. A break is needed because, as you can see in the visual, there is quite a bit of writing required on the building blocks.

Here is the procedure.

1. Model for students an idea that you are building. Put it in the top box. Ideally, use color coding (e.g., purple for the idea, pink for clarify, and light blue for support).

2. Then fill in other boxes from the bottom and work your way up (or they can fill in boxes from the top down). You don't need to do this in any order, though I often connect the boxes I fill in. If, for example, I clarify the evidence I just shared, I would write the evidence in a blue box (or use blue ink) and then write the clarification in a pink box above or next to it.

3. For a pre-conversation visual, model for students how to fill in as much as they can before they talk with a partner. But leave plenty of the bricks blank, because they will fill in more during and after the conversation.

4. Have students fill in boxes on their own visuals.

5. Have students talk with partners, but they should not write while talking. An observer-coach can do this, if desired.

6. Stop halfway through ("halftime") and have students write down notes from the conversation so far in the boxes, to build up their idea. While they do this, they can ask each other further clarify and support questions as needed. (For example, "What did you say about the main character?" "Remind me how we decided to define success?")

7. Ask students to talk again to finish their conversation, after which they put final notes into the bricks. Have them use pencil, and encourage them to erase, if needed, and to use question marks if they aren't sure, along with any other notations that help. What you don't want is for students to fill it in just to have filled it in. You want them to own it, and to see how an idea is born, grows, and changes over time. Remind them that even if their initial idea came from another student, from the teacher, or from the book, how they build it up over time will make it their own.

8. Optionally, you can have them meet with other partners who can help to fill in more bricks.

Here is a sample conversation from an eighth-grade history class. The prompt was, *Jefferson and Hamilton had very different views of the role of the federal government. Use these views to build up an idea that answers the question, "What should the government do?" and decide how effectively it did so (and still does).* Students had looked at primary and secondary sources and put notes on many of the bricks on their visuals, most of which were examples or quotations from the sources.

(1) A: What do you have on your bricks?

(2) B: Jefferson wanted the government to not do as much.

(3) A: What do you mean?

(4) B: He was, I mean, he wanted states to have more control. And he wanted to help the farmers. What do you have?

(5) A: I got a brick with that thing about farmers and states, and I got a brick that is, he thought that a strong government would be oppression, or tyr- tyranny.

(6) B: What about Hamilton?

(7) A: One brick it's, has he wanted to be more like England. He wanted more, like, the government to control everything.

(8) B: Like what?

(9) A: I got here a note about money, I think a big bank. He said they were collecting taxes, so they needed a bank or something like that.

(10) B: But Jefferson didn't want that. He didn't want to have, he didn't want to be like England again, like to have a king. And then/

(11) A: /But Washington didn't want to be a king.

(12) B: No, but he didn't want how England did things and, like raising taxes and all that, and telling us what to do. It's why the US wanted to fight to be free.

(13) A: I think maybe they were both kinda right. States should make, they should decide on what they need, like to help themselves. But the main government should do some decisions, too.

(14) B: Like?

(15) A: Like what to do with other countries, and the army, and wars.

(16) B: And laws. They do that, too.

(17) A: Wait, let me put that on a brick.

Notice how using bricks helped the students keep the conversation going and stay focused. Lines 1, 5, and 7 refer to evidence "bricks" that they had already made and needed some elaboration. Then they expanded the evidence in line 7 by noticing disagreement between Hamilton and Jefferson, which they synthesized into one brick, in line 17. This is a nice example of how conversations can build up ideas that weren't in either student's mind beforehand.

Stronger and Clearer Each Time Activity

This activity has students engage in successive pair-shares in which they improve their ideas and use of language each time they talk. Think of it as two or three pair-shares in a row, with some extra twists. The pre- and postwrite responses can clearly show the differences that the pair-shares create. To get students up out of their seats (which I almost always do, even in small rooms), you can have students get into conversation lines, which make the transitions less chaotic. You can have students work on a wide range of interpersonal communication skills in addition to supporting, such as clarifying, nonverbal communication, validating the ideas of others, and so on. Here is the procedure:

1. If there is time, have partners write their initial idea or ideas down on paper. This can help them build confidence and have more to say. And it can serve as a pre-assessment.

2. Pair students up. You can use any pairing strategy here, but I like to use a structure called conversation lines, in which two lines of students (A and B) face each other and interact. I prefer smaller lines because they fit better in tight classrooms (e.g., 3 facing 3, 4 facing 4).

3. Have line A talk first. Give them a minute or so, depending on the topic and the students' age. You can also have line B students ask a support or a clarify question to the partner (e.g., "Is there other evidence of that?" "What do you mean by . . .?"). I usually require these questions. Or, if their partner doesn't say much, line B students can even provide an idea seed by starting with, "What about . . ." Remind students that one of their jobs is to help their fellow students talk more about what they are learning and talk more academically during the year.

4. Use a sound (e.g., one ding on a chime) to change turns in a partnership. Now A listens while B talks.

5. When line B students are done, have all students tell one another, for ten seconds each, what information or ideas they will take with them to the next partner share. They can also take short notes between the two turns or before they switch to a new partner. They *should not* take notes during the talking.

6. Change the pairs so that all students now have a new partner. You can use a different sound cue (e.g., two dings) for moving one of the lines (the last student goes down the middle to the end of his or her own line). Line B students will share first this time. Before they start, remind them to borrow ideas and evidence and language from partners to make their ideas stronger and clearer for the next partner. If you don't model this and remind them often, they will tend to just say the same thing, or even less, each time.

7. After talking with and listening to three partners, have students write a postwrite response, without looking at the prewrite. Then they and you can compare the two writings to see how the talking made a difference and to see what you might need to work on next. Some teachers even have students highlight any language or ideas in their postwrites that they got from listening to their partners.

Next are some sample turns from one student in a ninth-grade English class. The prompt was, *How and why did Scout change during* To Kill a Mockingbird? *How did these changes contribute to a theme or life lesson?* A is the focal student, P1 is partner 1, P2 is partner 2, and so on, and T is the teacher.

(1)   A: I think she learned more about how to not judge people, you know, like not judge a book by its cover, like Boo Radley. *[Silence.]*

(2)   P1: Can you clarify the part about Boo Radley?

(3)   A: At first she thought Boo Radley was some kind of ghost, or a monster. Then little things happened, nice things that he did, like fix her clothes. And then he saved their lives. You know, from the mean drunk guy. And then I think//

(4)   T: //OK, line B, go.

(5)   P1: I think that about not judging people, too. And the mockingbird thing. All they do is sing and help people, so it's bad to kill them. My example is Tom Robinson. He helped people but cuz he was black, but people were racists and they killed him. They didn't believe him. But Atticus did.

(6)   A: What about Scout changing?

(7)   P1: I think she learns about racism by talking with her dad.

(8)   T: OK, take fifteen seconds apiece to tell your partner any ideas or evidence that they gave that you will use with your next partner.

(9)   A: I like what you said about Tom, how he helped people and was like a mockingbird.

(10) P1: I like what you said about not judge by what they look like.

(11) T: OK, now before you switch to a new partner, remember that your answer needs to be stronger and clearer than last time. OK, switch! Folks in line B begin.

(12) P2: I think she learns more about how people are brave. Like when Atticus he said *[reading notes]*, "I wanted you to see what real courage is, instead of getting the idea that courage is a man with a gun in his hand. It's when you know you're licked before you begin but you begin anyway and you see it through no matter what." *[Silence.]*

(13) A: You got any other evidence for courage?

(14) **P2:** My first partner said something about, um *[looks at notes]*, the sick lady, Ms. Du-something. She wanted to get off a drug, morphine, and not be addicted anymore. But I don't know//

(15) **T:** //OK, line A, go.

(16) **A:** I think Scout learned that people can be brave, even if they don't look like it. There are examples in the book. Like Boo Radley. She thought Boo Radley was some kind of ghost or bad man. Then he did nice things like fix her clothes. And even saved her life. And Atticus, too. I don't think she thought he was brave until he tried to get Tom free, and he stood up to the whole racist town people. And he knew he was going to lose, but did it anyway, like what he said in the quote you read.

Because of the length, I only included two partnerships instead of three. Yet, notice the idea building that happens even in these two turns by student A. Also notice the clarification moves and the extra supporting evidence that student A gains from his first two partners. And consider how a structured activity like this can help students improve their conversations.

Modified Whole-Class Discussions

We often think of whole-class discussions as opportunities to efficiently and accurately get content into kids' heads. Yet with modifications, they also have lots of potential for developing idea-building conversation skills. And some of these modifications might even improve content understandings as well.

Here are some suggestions for modifying whole-class discussions in order to engage in more and better idea building:

* Make sure the prompt focuses on building up an interesting and relevant idea or ideas.

* Make sure the prompt allows students to make some choices in how they build up ideas. Will students feel a sense of agency? Is there room for student insights, interpretations, opinions, and evidence? Or will they feel they are going through the motions of discussion, repeating what the teacher wants to hear, getting participation points, or saying the bare minimum?

- When a student poses an idea, encourage other students, rather than you, to respond with a clarification or support prompt. You might say, "Hmm. How might we build up that idea? You can prompt her to respond, or prompt the entire class, or add to the idea yourself."

- To encourage more students to talk during a whole-class discussion, have them turn to partners and build up the idea one-on-one as often as possible. Here are some sample prompts for partner talk:

  - OK, there's the prompt. Now brainstorm with partners what you think the most buildable idea is, and then, we will decide which one to build up.

  - Great idea, David! Let's turn to partners and tell one another what we might say next if David said that to us. You might add to what he said or ask for clarification or evidence, or something else. Partner B, you start.

  - Now that we have heard different pieces of evidence from others, I think it would help to tell your partner how we should decide which evidence is strongest. What criteria might we use?

  - Now that we have heard lots of clarifications and evidence on both sides, talk with your partner to decide which side weighs more, or which side has stronger evidence.

Here is a sample modified whole-class discussion from a fifth-grade science class. The prompt was, *Someone said that huge redwood trees, and all other plants, don't get their building material from the soil. They get it from the air. How can we explain and verify this?* The teacher had students start with a paired brainstorm session. Look for ways in which the teacher models conversation skills and pushes students to use them to help the entire group build up the idea, which is how to set up an experiment and then hypothesize based on possible results (T is the teacher).

(1)	T:	What are some ideas that came up in your paired brainstorming session? Alex?
(2)	A:	We, uh, thought that we could do an experiment. We measure the things at the start and after it grows.
(3)	T:	Any clarify or support questions for Alex and Eliana?
(4)	B:	What things are you going to measure?
(5)	E:	We'll measure the dirt, like weigh it.

(6)   C: In the ground? How do you weigh dirt in the ground?

(7)   A: So I think we'll put a seed in a pot. And we weigh it all. And watch it grow.

(8)   T: Let's build on Alex's and Eliana's experiment idea and make it our class idea for now. Now are there any other scientist questions about experiments like this?

(9)   F: So what causes what?

(10) S: I think we want to see if, if the dirt amount changes a lot. See if it's the same as what the plant weighs, like after it grows.

(11) T: OK, so let's assume we set up the experiment and six months later we weigh them both. What are the two possible outcomes, and what would they mean? Talk in pairs for a minute about this. *[One-minute pair-share.]*

(12) P: We think if the dirt doesn't change, you know, how much it weighs, and the plant is bigger, like it weighs more, then it didn't use the dirt to build, to grow.

(13) M: And if it does change, the dirt weight, the plant used it.

(14) T: Hmm. Let's say we find out that the dirt weight doesn't change. What can we hypothesize?

(15) W: Maybe it was the water?

(16) T: Could be, but let's say we take all the water out of the plant and it still weighs a lot.

(17) J: Maybe it's like that person said, from the air.

(18) K: How?

(19) Y: The air has stuff in it, like oxygen and . . ./

(20) N: /Carbon dioxide.

(21) T: So what do you find after you burn up logs in a fire?

(22) S: Charcoal.

(23) T: Which is carbon. So . . . ? Tell a partner what you think now. (*Pairs converse.*)

(24) V: My partner said that the plant has lots of carbon, and it comes from the carbon dioxide in the air. But we couldn't figure out how.

Notice how the teacher guides the conversation so that students do most of the thinking, but does not over-direct them. Also notice how the teacher prompts students to use conversation skills in lines 3 and 8, as well as scientific inquiry skills in lines 11, 14, and 23.

Creativity Conversations

This conversation activity is a bit more open-ended and real world. Its main emphasis is on developing student creativity, a skill that has been lacking in many classrooms in recent decades. It also helps students to learn and internalize the *creativity process*, which is also called *design thinking* in some contexts.

1. Pick a topic that requires a creative way to solve a problem or express a complex idea to others. Give options, if possible.

2. Model for students the collaborative creativity process. This process is not necessarily linear, but the steps generally go in this order:

   - Clarify the problem.

   - Brainstorm possible solution starters.

   - Narrow them down with critical thinking and criteria.

   - Zoom in on two and then compare their merits, limits, rationales, evidence, potentials, and related histories.

   - Choose the best solution and discuss how to implement it.

3. Have students collaborate to create or write their idea for a realistic audience.

Here is a sample conversation. The prompt in this fourth-grade English language arts class was, *Bullying is a problem at our school. How might we solve this? Remember to use the creativity process.*

(1)	A:	So it's about bullying, right? How to stop it.
(2)	B:	Yeah, it's being mean and picking on others.
(3)	A:	And making them feel bad or scared.
(4)	B:	OK, what are ideas to fix it?
(5)	A:	Maybe, kick 'em out of school?
(6)	B:	Or maybe have them get bullied by bigger people?

(7)	A:	Or they take a class or read a book, like, about how bullying is bad.
(8)	B:	OK, now we got three. But if we kick them out of school, what?
(9)	A:	A lot of kids'll have to leave school.
(10)	B:	OK with me.
(11)	A:	But they need to learn, too, and maybe they can change. And getting others to bully them, I don't think it'll help. They might get worse.
(12)	B:	So let's say the class or book idea. They can learn how it is bad.
(13)	A:	So they take a class after school, or they have to read a book about bullying.
(14)	B:	But how will the teachers know they read the book?
(15)	A:	Maybe they answer questions or something like that.

Notice the clarifying of the term *bullying* at the start. And notice the posing of different solution ideas (not just going with the first one posed), as well as some nice critiquing of ideas in lines 11, 12, and 14. I think you can see the power of having this type of conversation repeatedly, focused on various challenges and working with various partners, over the months and years.

Modified Jigsaw

Jigsaws provide students with a way to develop their idea-building skills. In typical jigsaws students think that their goal is just to fill in an information chart, but they *should* be trying to build up an important idea. They might still fill in a chart, but that is only a means to an end. The following modifications to the jigsaw procedure mean that students do more to expand their content understandings and language.

1. Divide up the text into three to six different sections. Plan to have the same number of students in a group as there are text sections.

2. Prepare a study guide that will help students become experts as they analyze and learn from a section of text. The study guide may have questions (open ended/under the surface), include a task, or be a graphic organizer to fill in (e.g., the Building Ideas Visual). Design it with the building up of one or more ideas in mind.

3. Strategically place students into their expert groups, and give them the text that each group will study.

4. In their expert groups, have students read the text and then discuss their conclusions, summaries, opinions, answers, task, or graphic organizer. They discuss how they will teach it to their colleagues in home groups.

5. Within the expert groups, in pairs, students practice what they will say with each other, twice. The first time the talker can use notes. The second time the talker doesn't use notes. After each time, the listening partner provides feedback and reminds the person practicing of any content or evidence that should be included to make the idea stronger. Then they switch roles.

6. Assign students, who are now experts, to home groups that combine experts on different sections. Each student orally shares their key information with the home group members. They have their notes, but they should try not to use them. Tell the members to try to come up with at least one clarify or support question each time someone shares.

7. Hold a class discussion to further synthesize, build, clarify, and support ideas that students discussed in their expert and home groups.

Skill 2—Pose Conversation-Worthy Ideas

The better that students are able to pose and select conversation-worthy (e.g., relevant, meaty, important) ideas, and the more they clarify and support these ideas, the better their conversations will support their learning. These ideas may come from the standards, curriculum guides, essential questions, subheadings in texts, student interests, and your own experience teaching your subject matter.

Here are just a few examples of ideas that students can build up in conversations:

- We need to make a graph of the two situations.
- I think Shayla became more humble in the story.
- The little birds were symbols of the freedom that she wanted to have.
- We need to think about bias when we use primary sources in history.
- All life needs water.
- Geography influences culture.
- Fractions, decimals, and percentages are similar but used for different reasons.
- I can use a baseball bat, a baseball, and a car to show Newton's three laws.
- The European explorers were motivated mostly by greed.
- The First Amendment doesn't do enough to protect us.
- We should cut it up into triangles and use the Pythagorean formula.

Notice that these ideas range in size, and not all of them are opinions. But all of them need more explanation, clarification, and support with evidence or detailed explanations. And all of them need at least a paragraph or more to describe them. In particular, most buildable ideas are *multifaceted, durable,* and *relevant.*

Multifaceted: This means that students bring different materials (ideas, evidence, definitions, opinions, values) to use for building the idea in conversations with one another. This can include different definitions of key terms, different pieces of evidence, different criteria for evaluating evidence, and so forth. Even if they do have the same pieces of evidence in their hands, they still should have different ways of describing or evaluating them (which often comes from a person's values) and how they support the main idea. So, if two students say the same thing, then it's not the type of idea we are looking for. And the final idea should vary, content-wise and linguistically, across students.

Durable: An idea should be buildable over time. This means that, with additional conversations, reading, reflection, and exposure to the idea, the idea can change and expand. Some ideas are lifetime ideas that build and change until we die. (For example, The United States is not a true democracy. To find the volume of an irregular object, you can dunk it in a measurable container of liquid. You need to learn from mistakes. The Earth is like a huge magnet.)

Relevant: The initial idea should be as relevant as possible to the prompt or purpose of the conversation. Even if the conversation starts with several brainstormed potential ideas, students should pick the one that is most relevant and useful for learning. They will be tempted to pick the most exciting one, but they need to stay on track with the prompt and topic of study. Remind students that it is OK to experiment and even play around with ideas, but there should always be an attempt to stay relevant. You can model this to the whole class by posing a variety of ideas and thinking aloud how you might choose the most relevant, buildable, and useful idea for conversation. This is well worth the time because, as you know, a weak, unbuildable, or irrelevant idea from the start can greatly hinder productive conversation.

Notice this focus on relevance in the next snippet from a tenth-grade world history conversation. Students had been analyzing a chart with the World War I financial costs and death tolls by country. The prompt was, *How might these statistics affect the attitudes of these countries after World War I? Pick an idea to focus on that could become a key point in a treaty that you will help write.* After this conversation, students compared their key points to those in the Treaty of Versailles.

(1)   A: What are some ideas?

(2)   B: These countries here lost billions of dollars and probably wanted it back. I think/

(3)   A: /And the millions of lives, too. You can't pay those back.

(4)   B: Yeah, no. And Germany and Austria lost even more money. So I don't think they had any money to pay back.

(5)   A: Yeah. But they should.

(6)   B: Yeah. But what about the regular people? I don't think a lot of people even wanted a war. Like out in small towns. Should they pay?

(7)   A: No. So, all that money and all those people dead! Why do people think they need to take over the world? Why do they let crazy people be leaders?

(8)   B: Yeah, and they should be put in jail for starting it.

(9)   A: And another thing is the military. Germany and Austria shouldn't have one so they, like, can't attack again. Right?

(10) B: OK. So what idea is good for talking more?

(11) A: We just talked. That wasn't enough?

(12) B: No. We gotta focus on one thing and build it up. And it needs to answer the question.

(13) A: OK. I think maybe the regular people idea.

(14) B: OK. The treaty shouldn't punish them, but it should punish the leaders who started it all.

(15) A: So, how?

Notice that when student A thought this was enough talk, student B reminded her that they had been brainstorming and that they still needed to build up an idea in the conversation.

Even though you want students to come up with their own ideas, you should have some seedling ideas in your pocket that you can give to students when they need them. Your idea seeds can be informed by the standards, curriculum materials, and your students. You can have students start with these ideas, or you can listen in on conversations and provide them when necessary.

The following instructional activity can help students come up with and select the most buildable ideas for their conversations.

Key Words in an Envelope

This is a fun and creative activity to come up with ideas from the key words and terms that students need to use. Pick some key terms for building up a major idea for the unit. Write three to six of these key words or expressions on cards and put them in envelopes to give to pairs or groups of students. Have students organize the terms however they want, such as in a semantic web, in categories, in a sequence, in a paragraph that has added words or sentences from students' minds, on a picture that they draw, in a mini-skit, or in some other representation. You can add cards over time to the envelopes, and students can also add cards to their evolving representations of the idea.

For example, a sixth-grade teacher teaching the growth of civilizations put the words *agriculture, food surplus, division of labor*, and *civilization* on four different cards. After two introductory lessons that helped to familiarize (but not concretize) the meanings of the terms, she asked, *How do these terms relate to one another? Talk about how they fit together, and come up with an engaging and clear way to present your idea. Remember, as you talk, to push one another to clarify and support ideas.*

Here is a sample conversation from this lesson.

(1)   A: So, agriculture is farming, like growing food, right?

(2)   B: Yeah.

(3)   A: And food surplus is extra food, like when farmers grow more than they eat.

(4)   B: OK. That's two cards.

(5)   A: But what is division of labor?

(6)   B: I think when they get different jobs. So when you don't . . . aren't a farmer.

(7)   A: What do you mean?

(8)   B: I think way before, everyone was a farmer. But when they made extra food, the surplus, maybe you don't like farming, so you make tools and sell them.

(9)   A: So let's put 'em together.

(10) B: So they got better at agriculture and they did *[placing the cards in a line]*, they had a food surplus. And cuz of more food, the people had division of labor cuz they could buy food.

(11) A: Why?

(12) B: The tool guy sells tools and has money.

(13) A: They had money?

(14) B: I don't know. Maybe they traded stuff. But people had other jobs cuz they can buy food.

(15) A: What about the civilization card?

(16) B: And they got civilization cuz you need lots of different jobs to be a civilization. Now what?

(17) B: We make a poster or something. Or we could, maybe we act it out, cuz it's faster and more fun.

Notice the ownership of the key terms and the clarification of them because students used them to build up a bigger idea in a cause-and-effect sequence. And the conversation both prepared and motivated them to do more than the bare minimum on the final product. And yet, the idea that they came up with in line 16 is just the beginning. It requires other skills to build it up, one of which is clarification, which is Skill 3.

Skill 3—Clarify

Clarifying means working with partners to establish meanings that are clear enough to do all the things needed to have a productive conversation. In the conversation that follows, for example, if in line 2 student B had said, "OK," without really understanding what A had said in line 1, then the conversation might have stopped. Students also need to clarify how evidence supports the idea, what a key term means, why they value certain types of evidence, why something is important or not, and so on. Look for clarifying that builds up an idea in the following fifth-grade conversation, prompted by the question, *Did Paul Revere play a significant role in the American Revolution?*

(1) A: I think yes.

(2) B: Why?

(3) A: Cuz he warned those people about the British soldiers.

(4) B: Yeah. But is that enough to like help us win the Revolution?

(5) A: I think so. Remember it said it gave them time to surprise the British? I think that helped them win.

(6) B: But that was just a battle. The war was a lot bigger.

(7) A: I don't know. Maybe//

(8) B: //Maybe it gave them more, like, confidence for other battles. It was, it was early, and I don't know if they thought they could beat the real soldiers, the British ones.

(9) A: So you think it got them like pumped up for more fight?

(10) B: Yeah. Maybe like a basketball team that just started out. They win a game or two and it gets them to work hard and do more, you know.

Both students helped to clarify the initial idea of Revere playing a significant role in the Revolution. They both asked questions, they both added clarifying turns, and they both ended up with a more solid idea even after just a handful of turns. It is important to push students to do more clarifying than they think is necessary. They tend to think that everything that they say, which is often the bare minimum, is clearly understood by whoever is listening. So, to help them, you can model and scaffold the following moves that are commonly used to clarify ideas in a conversation.

- **Ask questions** ("Why did you say that . . . ? How did . . . ? Does that mean . . . ?")
- **Define** a term used. ("What does *truth* mean?" "How would you define *patriot*?")
- **Elaborate** on a basic idea. ("Tell me more about why you think . . . ?") Often, a student will respond in a statement without much detail. For example, "We need to learn history so we don't make the same mistakes." Students can ask for elaboration by saying, "Tell me more about . . ." And we should teach students to ask others to elaborate on something specific, rather than just, "Can you elaborate?" because it forces the prompter to pick out a certain piece of what the speaker has said and name it. For example, "Can you elaborate on what history is and what counts as a mistake in history?"
- **Paraphrase** one or more turns and then condense them back to the partner. ("So what you are saying is that more supply of stuff lowers the demand for it?")

Purposes for paraphrasing include to

- keep track of what you are hearing,

- describe what the partner just said in your own words,

- check to see whether what you heard was the talker's intended message,

- organize the partner's points,

- help the partner and the conversation stick to the topic and build the intended idea,

- chunk and highlight key information to make it more memorable (as we do in reading).

- **Use analogies, drama, and visual aids** (e.g., semantic map, Venn diagram, chart, graph). Visuals are the most commonly used strategies from this list, but it also helps to be able to dramatize ideas and use analogies. (For example, *A cell is like a school.*)

As you can see, clarifying comes in many forms. Even though it's not always needed, (for example, when two students already have similar enough meanings in their minds), it is usually needed. So, it is better to err on the side of over-clarification. Here are some activities to help students improve their clarifying.

Paraphrase Practice

Practicing can help students to improve their paraphrasing. Here is the procedure:

1. Have student pairs, have students listen to long conversational turns. You might say or even read these to them.

2. Have them turn to a partner to paraphrase what they heard from you.

3. You can have A and B partners alternate, or they can paraphrase the same message and synthesize their ideas into a final paraphrase.

4. Have them start with phrases such as "I think I understand. You said . . ." or "So, in other words . . ." or "So what you are saying is . . ." Remind them that listening to the key information is vital for paraphrasing—and remember to model how to listen for key information. Table 2.2 depicts a sample chart that you can use or show to help students practice.

IF YOU SAY . . .	I'LL PARAPHRASE BY SAYING
It takes a long time to travel to other stars. And they might be like our sun with planets like Earth. I think there is life out there and that maybe they have visited here, but I don't know how they figured out how to stay alive that long. Because it takes light like thousands of years to get here, so to get there, we gotta have a ship that travels faster than light, and we don't have that. I don't know when that'll happen. I saw a show on wormholes, but I don't know if they are real.	So what you're saying is that stars are suns and might have planets around them. And they are far enough away that we would take thousands of years to travel to them, or more, because we don't have spaceships fast enough.
She says to her son that her life has been really hard, but she keeps on going. Like, she doesn't give up at all. She keeps on walking up the stairs. They don't have carpet. I don't think she's rich because that would be a crystal stair, right? And the tacks are like nails, I think, and they hurt. I don't think I would keep going up those stairs. What's at the top? Why keep going? I don't know.	What I heard was that you think that the poem is about the lady telling her son to keep going, even if life is really hard, and even if you don't know what the future will be like.
In this story, all the kids come over in a rainbow-colored station wagon. They pull up in front of the house, jump out, and hug everyone from the kitchen to the living room. All summer they tended the garden and ate up all the strawberries and melons. They play lots of musical instruments. When they finally left, everyone was sad. But they knew the relatives would be back next summer. They seemed to love each other.	So, in other words, the story is about a loving family. When the relatives drive up to visit, they jump out of their car and hug everyone. The family spends the summer together eating, playing, and making music.

Table 2.2 Paraphrase practice examples

Two or More Connected Sentences

Most students need to get into the habit of orally expressing their ideas with more than one sentence. This is more of a student practice, or habit, to use across most activities than it is a specific activity. Tell students that any time they answer a question, to the whole class or a peer, they have to try to use at least two sentences. The first sentence will usually be a topic sentence, claim, or general statement. The second sentence (and any others) will clarify or support the first sentence. You can also stipulate what you want the second sentence to do. You might say that it needs to be a support sentence or a clarify sentence.

In response to the question, *What was the author's purpose for writing this article?* a student may say, "It's about tides," for her initial idea. Teachers should model how to add additional sentences to clarify this: *This article is about tides. Tides are when the ocean moves and water comes up and down. Tidal change is caused mostly by the moon's gravity pulling on the water.* Note that you can also use this practice to strengthen the next skill of supporting ideas with evidence.

Skill 4—Support Ideas

Supporting an idea means to back it up with evidence, examples, and reasoning. Evidence comes in different forms: examples from texts, results from surveys, conclusions from research, statistics, and personal accounts, to name a few. Evidence ranges in terms of its quality and how well it supports an idea. Students need to learn how to find, use, and evaluate the strength of evidence in order to build up ideas as much as possible. The activities in this chapter are meant to help.

In many cases, students need both inductive and deductive skills for using evidence. With inductive thinking, they identify the evidence first and begin to form ideas that the evidence supports. This means they look at events, dialogues, symbols, and data to notice patterns that lead to the formation and support of an idea. This tends to be more common when reading fiction, looking at patterns in math and history, and engaging with certain types of discovery science tasks.

For deductive thinking, students start with an idea or a claim and look for evidence that supports it. This is common in expository articles and argument-based messages. First, students need to identify the main idea, thesis, or claim. Then they go through the text or texts, looking for and evaluating the evidence given by the author/speaker.

There are four main types of evidence that can be used, either inductively, deductively, or both, during academic conversations.

1. **Evidence from the text.** Most standards highlight the importance of evidence from the texts that students are reading and using to learn. Make sure, though, that students know *why* they are supposed to use text evidence. Often if you ask them, they will say, "Because we have to" or something similar. Make sure students know that using text-based evidence is a powerful way to build up their ideas now and in the future.

2. **Evidence from other texts.** Many ideas are not confined to just one text. You should encourage students to use evidence from texts that they have read this year, last year, at home, and so forth. They can also use examples from additional texts they may have encountered, such as web pages, TV shows, movies, and works of art. Remember to add extra doses of critical literacy when using some of these sources of evidence (e.g., model how to evaluate the trustworthiness of the source).

3. **Evidence from the world.** We must train and motivate students to be continually observing what is going on in the world. And we must help them make links between the real world and the classroom. You likely have lesson plans with extension activities, which often include looking for examples in the real world.

4. **Evidence from one's own life**. Students (and adults) often find it easiest to share evidence and examples from their own lives, but this can sometimes cause them to veer from the conversation's purpose. They need to practice thinking about whether the evidence from their lives is truly helpful.

While there will be exceptions, a good default mode is for students to give and ask for evidence in the order presented in the previous list. It is often easier for them to jump straight to number 4, but I usually encourage students to use text-based evidence first. Text-based evidence gets students into the text, which usually has accurate and valuable information as well as the academic language that we want students to be immersed in.

Students shouldn't just pick the first three things that vaguely "fill in the blanks" of evidence. Students need modeling, apprenticing, and lots of discussion about what makes evidence strong and what makes it weak. They also need lots of work on how to objectively evaluate and compare the strengths of evidence and ideas.

So, how does a student figure out if one piece of evidence is stronger than another piece of evidence? One way is through conversations. Conversations allow students to try out and discuss their evidence—how strong or weak it is—with others. Over time, conversations immerse students in the thinking it takes to evaluate strong and weak evidence in academic settings and beyond. For example, over time students might learn that a family member's reasons and evidence supporting the side of an argument aren't very strong.

Notice how the skill of supporting is honed in the following sixth-grade conversation, which was prompted by, *What was the author's purpose in writing* The Giver?

(1) A: I think *The Giver* is about showing how bad humans can be, and that we need to know about that bad stuff.

(2) B: Why?

(3) A: Because all those bad memories the Giver has, of war and death. You know. Like on page 120 he says, "Overwhelmed by pain, he lay there in the fearsome stench for hours, listened to the men and animals die, and learned what warfare meant."

(4) B: So, why remember those things?

(5) A: So we don't do that stuff again. So like we don't do war and make people suffer.

(6) B: I think I kinda agree with that, but I don't think kids should know all of those things till they grow up. They don't start wars.

(7) A: I agree. Maybe that's why they had a Giver. If they didn't, maybe they'd start new wars. Maybe they/

(8) B: /Yeah, we need to learn from mistakes. Like our history, we got world wars, they kill innocent people, and terror, terrorism.

(9) A: And we spend all that money on bombs and planes and the army, and we could spend it on homeless people and maybe other stuff like/

(10) B: /Like medicine, right?

(11) A: Yeah.

(12) B: OK, but which bad things should we know?

(13) A: You mean like which stuff'll help us, keep us from doing terrible things?

(14) B: Bombs, nuclear bombs, you know, and war.

(15) A: And I also think fighting, when people hurt others.

Notice the examples from the text and from the world the students used to build up their idea. Then, ideally, these students would have additional conversations with other students about the same topic to further build their ideas. Here are some activities to help you help your students improve the skill of supporting ideas.

Evidence and Non-evidence

This activity, adapted from Beck, McKeown, and Kucan (2013), gives students a chance to practice their abilities to evaluate the strength and relevance of different pieces of evidence in support of an idea. Instead of the yes/no method outlined below, you can have them use a continuum that has the words *strong* on one side and *not at all* on another. Students then put the cards somewhere on the continuum and argue for why they chose that spot.

1. Show students an idea statement, such as *We shouldn't clone humans*.

2. Give students cards with evidence, reasons, non-examples, poor evidence, and nonrelated ideas.

3. Students discuss and choose which cards strongly support the statement. For example, "Biologically, each person was meant to be unique" and "One survey of average Americans shows that 72% of them oppose cloning of humans" might support it to varying degrees, while "Cloning means making a biological copy of an organism" and "Cloning might provide ways to cure serious illnesses" wouldn't support it.

4. Students can also come up with evidence and non-evidence cards.

Back It Up

This activity offers much-needed practice in supporting one's claims and reasons with solid evidence—not just any evidence. It shows students the different types of evidence that exist and lets them evaluate the relative strength of each. Here is the procedure:

1. Put up samples of ideas and model how to find, use, and evaluate the different types of support. Notice that some of these examples are stronger than others in supporting the main claim. The sample topic in Table 2.3 comes from a seventh-grade science class.

2. Have pairs read an article and use a chart like Table 2.3 to analyze and evaluate the quality of the evidence and reasoning used. Encourage them to say things such as "I liked the detailed and heartfelt quotation from, but that is just one person, and I need to hear from more people . . . "

3. Have students choose a topic that they are interested in, pose an idea or claim, and fill in their own chart (see Table 2.3). They can add additional columns. They don't need to come up with evidence for every row, but it helps for them to be on the lookout for it, and to think about how a certain missing type of evidence might help strengthen the idea at the top. Vehemently encourage them to see the chart as a tool to come up with the strongest evidence possible to build up their ideas—not just another chart to fill in for points.

TYPE OF SUPPORT	EVIDENCE FOR SUPPORTING THE IDEA: "It's not worth it to use mefloquine to prevent contracting malaria."
FACT/STATISTIC	The American Society of Health System Pharmacists says that mefloquine can cause serious side effects and potentially long-term mental health problems such as depression, hallucinations, and anxiety and neurological side effects such as poor balance, seizures, and ringing in the ears.
QUOTE FROM AN EXPERT	Ultimately, we must address the issue presented by Marianne Stevens, chief spokesperson for the WHO: "It is getting increasingly difficult to reduce the contraction of malaria without using more toxic prophylactic substances."
QUOTE FROM A PERSON INVOLVED	A traveler to Nepal said, "We don't want to get malaria, but we keep getting crazy nightmares and other weird side effects."
CITATION FROM CREDIBLE SOURCE	In a recent WHO report, researchers estimated that certain strains of malaria will become totally resistant to current preventative medicines within the next five years.
EXAMPLE	Last November, a high number of travelers with strange symptoms were brought to local health clinics. All had been using mefloquine to prevent malaria.
ANECDOTE	On a recent trip to Nepal, I contracted malaria even though I was using mefloquine.
COMPARISON	This is similar to using certain types of radiation to cure cancer. The radiation often does unforeseeable harm to certain parts of the body.
ANALOGY	Can mosquitoes be spies? It seems like every attack strategy we have, mosquitoes and their parasites quickly adapt.

Table 2.3 Types of support for ideas (with examples)

Information Gap Cards

In information gap activities, students need to talk and listen in order to bridge information gaps. A jigsaw is a common example. Students need to share their knowledge (which often includes evidence, examples, reasons, and clarifications) with others to accomplish a task. Often the task involves filling in an organizer that is missing information. For example, form A is missing information that student B has, and vice versa.

You can also give students information cards that they use to become experts in whatever is on the card. This helps improve the skill of supporting ideas with evidence because students are mostly gathering information in the form of evidence and examples from other students. And, yes, students should ask clarifying questions to work on their clarifying skills as they listen to partners share.

SNOWSHOE HARE

Habitat: mountain forests with lots of shrubs

Diet: leaves, grass, bark, buds, twigs

Dangers: lynx, bobcat, fox, coyote, owl, puma

Adaptations: white fur in winter and brown in summer; big feet for the snow; big ears to hear predators; mostly nocturnal (I come out and look for food at night)

Figure 2.3 Sample information gap

For example, you might make (or have students make) four different cards with unique animal adaptations on them. Use four different colors for the cards. Create a fifth card that you use as a model. The prompt might be, *You are thinking of moving to the habitat where your partner lives. Ask him or her how you can adapt in order to survive.* Here is the rest of the procedure:

1. Model for students how to respond to the prompts (in step 3) with your animal card. "For example, I am a snowshoe hare and I live in mountain forests. I prefer to eat grass and leaves, but in the winter I eat bark and twigs because that's all I can find. To avoid my many predators, I turn white in the winter to blend in with the snow, and brown in the summer to match the dirt. I also use my big ears to hear those pesky predators, and my big feet are especially helpful in the snow to get away. They're like snowshoes. For example, the other day a bobcat tried to chase me and when I looked back, he was chest deep in the snow. Did I go back to help him? Not." Act out or explain words they will need to know and use (*infrasonic, echolocation, nocturnal*, etc.).

2. Students read their own cards and try to remember the information. They don't show the cards to others.

3. Students meet with their first partner (who is a different animal). They should become the animal and talk in the first person. They say the animal that they are right off the bat (it's not a guessing game). As they share, they can peek at their own cards, if needed, but challenge them to use their cards very little, if at all, especially when they share with the final partner. You can provide questions and response starters such as

   - What are you?

   - Where do you live?

   - How have you adapted to eat what you eat? (Because I eat _____, I have _____.)

   - How have you adapted to avoid dangers? One trait that helps me avoid . . .

   - Can you clarify . . .? Can you give an example of . . .? (For example, one time I _____.)

4. Remind students that the goal is to build up their ideas about adaptation, not just answer questions. They can take notes, but after the person talks, not during. Challenge them not to look at the questions and response starters the third time.

5. They meet with the other two animals and learn how they would need to adapt to survive in each of their habitats. As they build confidence, they can use the card less and even add some extra pizzazz to the sharing (within reason). "For example, one time this big ole leopard was getting near me and my calves. I could see him, so I made sure I kept a safe distance. Then I used my special infrasonic ability to warn my calves without anyone else hearing it."

6. Have a class discussion that synthesizes the idea (of animal adaptation, in this case).

Conclusion

Effective conversations build one or more ideas as much as possible. All partners in a conversation should be trying to build up at least one idea, and they need to use the skills of clarifying and supporting (Skills 3 and 4) as appropriate. As they work together to help each other build up robust ideas in their minds, their confidence and sense of agency increase. They are proud of what they build, and they feel that they own it, as opposed to just memorizing someone else's ideas to get points on a test. Moreover, clarifying and supporting require copious amounts of language and thinking, which grow as students interact.

But, you might be thinking, not all conversations build just one idea. What about arguments? In arguments, you need to build up two or more competing ideas and then evaluate and compare their strengths to choose one, which is Skill 5, the focus of the next chapter.

Chapter 3

Collaborative Arguments

Even though it's the much less traveled path,
let us argue in ways that lead us to truth,
growth, and progress.

When you think of argumentation, you might picture people raising their voices, trying to win an argument at all costs. You might think of a heated debate or a courtroom case.

Collaborative argumentation is different. First, it's not about winning. Partners don't pick a side and then fight for it no matter how strong the other side's evidence is: rather, they focus on getting to the truth and making the best choice. Second, it's collaborative, which means that students work together during the conversation to build up *all* the sides, before choosing one. They might end up choosing different sides, but they work together throughout the conversation.

For these reasons, the focal conversation skill of this chapter is evaluating evidence, which includes objectively and logically deciding, negotiating, or agreeing to disagree with respect to which side has the strongest support. Good evaluating, of course, depends on how well students built up the two or more competing ideas (i.e., how well they followed the skills in Chapter 2).

As you already know, argumentation often fosters increased engagement during lessons—and life, right? There is energy that results from the tension between two ideas, like a basketball game between rival teams. As in a basketball game, before an argument unfolds we are not entirely sure which side will win or how it will play out. Whichever side is chosen, teachers usually see the learning value, especially when students follow collaborative norms.

One of the worst habits that people have when arguing is to start off by taking a side and then not helping at all to build up the opposite side. For example, I might think that we should bring back extinct species such as dinosaurs. Now, in my mind, I might also have some evidence and reasons that support the opposing side, but I don't share it because I want to win so badly. Yet, to truly collaborate, I should share all the information that I have and try to build up both ideas as much as possible, parking my opinion in the back of my mind as much as possible, and I should respect the opposing side all along the way as much as possible.

I heard one teacher say, "Try not to pre-pick a side, but if you do, hide it as well as you can until the end. And be willing to change your initial opinion if the other side's evidence weighs more." This collaborative, "wait until you have all the information" mentality will serve students well in school and beyond.

Skill 5—Evaluating the Quality of Evidence and Reasoning

Evaluating, in this chapter, means assigning different values to evidence, which includes examples and reasoning that support a side of an argument. Once my partner and I have built up both sides of the argument (using conversation skills 1 through 4 in Chapter 2) of, let's say, whether to build new nuclear power plants, we work together to weigh each side by evaluating the evidence. We could just eyeball it or use our gut reactions, but eyeballs and guts tend to be unreliable and inconsistent over time. It's much more academic to strive to use criteria objectively to assign values to evidences in order to compare them.

A criterion is a rule or principle used to judge the value or logic of something (e.g., evidence). In our communication with others, we must try to agree on the criteria that we use, and then we must try to agree on how the information matches up with, or is described by, the criteria. For example, when I evaluate the ramifications of cutting down trees in the rain forest, I use the criteria of short- and long-term financial gains, water runoff, loss of habitat, loss of potential medicines, and the ethics involved in each.

Sometimes the criteria are straightforward and even quantifiable. We might say, "This will take more time than that." "This item costs more money than that item." "Both appear to be of the same quality." Yet, in much of school (and life), we must grapple with subjective issues, evidence, and reasons. We must often compare apples to oranges, so to speak. We might, for instance, be asked to evaluate the contributions of a historical person such as Christopher Columbus. What value did his actions have for the world or certain groups of people? He started the colonization and trade between the Americas and Europe. Yet, slavery was also a product of his "discovery." And millions of Native Americans died in the years following his arrival. Did he do more harm than good? Should we no longer celebrate Columbus Day? Answering these types of questions requires evaluation of very different types of subjective ideas.

Criteria are derived from a variety of sources: teachers, classrooms, school systems, governmental agencies, parents, and a person's own background experience and culture. And these variables, as you might guess, tend to vary from one person to the next. In collaborative argumentation, the criteria used to evaluate are rational, common-denominator categories that must be understood and agreed on by the partners in the conversation. (By contrast, in a dictatorial setting, the dictator, or boss, decides the criteria, however irrational they might be.) Therefore, criteria need to be negotiated to a large extent by both parties involved. Student A needs to at least agree that student B's use of criteria is logical and plausible, or whatever A proposes will mean little to B. For example, student A may decide to evaluate the quality of a movie. If B does not agree on the criteria used to determine quality, such as plot, character development, and special effects, then both may disagree, and the conversation may fizzle out.

Our students need to understand the many ways in which the world evaluates things. They must be able to understand how various people in various settings use criteria to assess the worth of something. Being a good employee means more than satisfying the criterion of being on time and staying late. One must also be professional, dress a certain way, relate to others, and be productive. Likewise, people of different fields (e.g., politics, medicine, history, law, education, technology) tend to have their own criteria for evaluating evidence and ideas, and students need to learn those criteria in order to better understand those disciplines. Of course, students must continue to develop their own ways of evaluating life's wide array of valuable ideas and evidence.

Because the use of criteria are unfamiliar to many students, give minilessons that introduce and model their use. I start with, "What are criteria?" We then discuss how criteria are like requirements with different levels and degrees. Then I move on to the use of evidence and examples, which I put up on a poster that evolves during the year.

Many criteria are used to evaluate and compare evidence, as well as decisions based on this comparing. Here are just a few of the more popular ones, which I put in question form. These criteria questions can have scales, which you will see in the activities that follow.

- **How much money does it require?** What will it cost? Knowing the cost of something makes it possible to start weighing whether the benefits are worth it. Is a measure that leads to better health, for example, worth the money invested?
- **Do long-term benefits outweigh short-term negatives?** Or vice versa? Long-term positives and negatives must be considered and evaluated fairly against the short-term ones.
- **What will be the likely future impact of either side?** It's important to check on what we think may happen as a result of the decision. Ideally, we would be able to refer to similar situations as evidence.
- **How beneficial or harmful to health is it?** Both mental and physical health are major criteria that we want to try to maximize.
- **How beneficial or harmful is it to the environment?** It's vital to make decisions that look after our one and only planet. Many species are extinct because of greedy and short-term decisions.
- **How ethical, moral, just, and respectful of human rights is it?** These mean doing what is right and letting people do what they deserve to do as humans. Students must develop the abilities to decide what is right and wrong by measuring it with one of the greatest and most subjective yardsticks of all: What is the better of the two options for the individuals involved and for society?
- **How much time does it take? How valuable is time?**
- **What is the potential loss or gain of human lives?** How many people could be helped?
- **How credible is the source?** How much bias might there be in the source of the evidence?

The more subjective and abstract the criteria are, the more modeling and practice the students will need in using them to evaluate.

The beauty and challenge of evaluation is that people tend to differ in how they evaluate because they have different values. These differences fuel highly rich conversations because students need *to try to come to an agreement* on how to assign value or weight to the evidence on a side. They seldom will agree completely, but it is in the trying that we see wonderfully crafted ideas, evidence, explanations, negotiation, and uses of academic language.

Take a look at the following conversation excerpt in an eighth-grade English language arts class. After reading articles on the topic of social media's value to society, the teacher asked, *Now decide with your partner if social media is more negative or positive for society. Make sure to use criteria to evaluate the strength of your evidence.* After they came up with evidence on each side, they talked about which side was better supported (i.e., was heavier or stronger) overall.

---

(1)   A: So why is the not good side heavier?

(2)   B: One thing is people get news from it. Some of it's real, but a lot of it's fake. I think it's better to not know news than, like, to learn the fake stuff.

(3)   A: Yeah. And like most people don't sign up for Facebook for the news. But there it is, in their face every day. A lot of it's fake.

(4)   B: And social media takes a lot of time. I know people with hundreds of friends. They could be doing other things, and/

(5)   A: /And research here says heavy users aren't good at talking with others, like talking in real life.

(6)   B: Now, the other side?

(7)   A: The good of it is cuz it lets people communicate far away, like who live in other places.

(8)   B: What criteria?

(9)   A: Relationships.

(10) B: Can you explain?

(11) A: People don't have time to meet at places or on the phone. So they see how their friends far away are doing. They look at pictures and videos. And here in the article, 90 percent of adults use Facebook for relationships and 70 percent of teenagers say social media connects to friends.

(12) B: And Twitter can keep you connecting without taking a lot of time.

(13) A: So let's say it's bad if you use it too much. But maybe if you don't have too many friends and don't use up lots of hours in a day, maybe it's OK to build relationships.

(14) B: OK.

Even though this is just an excerpt, we can see the powerful thinking that students were doing as they thought about criteria and compared evidence on both sides. As you can see, a lot of the use of criteria depends on what people value. I might value face-to-face conversation, while you might value online connectedness with a much larger group of people. As we talk, we can evaluate, compare, and negotiate—all of which gets us to think more deeply and use language in a variety of powerful ways.

Recognizing and Avoiding Persuasive Techniques, Faulty Logic, and Bias

Persuasive techniques. It is helpful to go over the common persuasive tactics that advertisers and others (like politicians) use to persuade people to make illogical and uninformed decisions. Such techniques include the use of misleading statistics, appeals to authority (e.g., doctors recommend . . .), bandwagon appeals (e.g., everyone believes this and so should you), clever slogans, emotional language, exaggerated metaphors and analogies, hyperbole, promotions by famous people, the common person appeal, and attributing a cause to a factor that is merely correlational. For example, an author might find that more lunch consumed correlates to higher reading comprehension scores in an elementary school. Does that mean that eating more improves reading? Students must be trained to see around this type of faulty logic, starting in elementary grades.

Students, even early on, start to formulate their opinions about the world. They start deciding who they are, what they stand for, and what they will fight for, mostly figuratively but sometimes even literally. They realize that others want to persuade them to be a certain way and to think certain things. They must start thinking about how some of the decisions they make now can help or hinder who they want to be and maybe affect them forever.

Faulty logic. When appropriate, teach students to notice various types of faulty reasoning that people often use to support their opinions. Some reasoning fallacies include the following:

- *False analogies*—Using a common illustration that seems similar but does not match up in important areas. For example, the mind is often compared to an advanced computer, but there are many important differences.
- *False causality*—Attributing an effect to a cause without evidence. "In babies the growth of hair comes before the growth of teeth, so hair growth is needed for growing teeth."
- *False logic*—Arguing that a point is true because its opposite cannot be proved. For example, "Since there is no evidence of foul play here, it was just a coincidence" doesn't mean there was no foul play.

- *Weak generalization*—Using too few examples to make a claim or to draw a conclusion. "After reading about all those crooked politicians in the news, I think they are all corrupt."
- *Appeal to emotion*—Using emotional language and feeling as justifiable proof of a claim. For example, "Most rational people would agree that all people who use plastic bags don't care about all the innocent sea animals that suffer horrible deaths from them."
- *Fluff*—Using large amounts of text or talk to give the appearance of large quantities of evidence, even though it does not prove or support anything.

We need to prepare students to be able to (a) talk about and critique examples of faulty logic in texts that they read, (b) identify when others use them in conversations, and (c) avoid using them in their own thinking, talking, and writing. Students can respond to others with comments such as these: "I still would like some more evidence that supports it." "That analogy breaks down pretty quickly. For example . . ." "That seems more like correlation rather than causation. How did the ___ cause the effect?" "That is a sad story, but I would like some more hard evidence." "Please boil it down to the evidence that . . ."

Bias. Bias is all around. Bias usually means that you include only certain facts, use language that favors a certain perspective, or make something or someone look better than they really are. People who have opinions often exclude or downplay any evidence or reasoning that they don't agree with. Bias isn't the same as opinion. I might have a well-informed opinion in which I have looked at both sides, and, because I value certain things more than others, I take a side. Bias is when I purposely don't include contradictory information or I use loaded language that tends to influence others to my side to prevent them from making objective decisions. For example, most news networks tend to be biased toward a certain side of the political spectrum, choosing stories and words that support their side.

Conversations can help students see the bias in others and in themselves. By talking with others and building up all sides of an issue objectively, their ideas can be vetted by others. When the classroom culture is focused on the truth and building ideas in objective ways, students challenge one another to see their biases and confront them. Student A might share with her partner all of the advantages of using social media and not share any disadvantages. Her partner can then challenge her to come up with as many disadvantages as possible and then explain why, in her opinion, social media is better than other activities.

Practicing the Language of Argumentation in a Conversation

At times during conversation activities, it helps to zoom in on certain uses of language that help to clarify the various steps in the argumentation process. Table 3.1, with steps on the left-hand side and language samples on the right-hand side, can help you model and scaffold different ways of describing the various components and skills needed for effective argumentation. When you observe students, look for strengths and needs with respect to these steps, and reinforce or model them when appropriate. Students can also benefit from creating and looking at different variations of Table 3.1.

STEPS	WHAT STUDENTS MIGHT SAY FOR THESE STEPS
1. Explain how the evidence supports a given side.	• This evidence supports the no side because it shows how the character felt about her aunt. • Because in the lab there was a change in color, it means that it was a reaction because . . .
2. Build up all sides of the argument with clarifying and supporting. Keep track of the evidences.	• Do you have any other evidence to build up this side? • I think we need to build up the opposite claim now. • I think we should build up the second side more.
3. Poke holes in the evidences. Show their weaknesses.	• OK, a weakness of this evidence is that the numbers are only from a survey done in one state, not the whole United States.
4. Decide on (and negotiate) the criteria to be used to evaluate the weight or strength of evidence.	• What criteria should we use? • Let's make sure to compare overall costs, money spent. • We could use long-term results and short-term results. • We could use the credibility of the authors.
5. Evaluate the total strength of the evidence on each side, compare claims, and choose the strongest or heaviest one.	• So, after poking holes in some of these, when we add them all up together on each side, I think this side is heavier, based on the following criteria. • This side is stronger because, in the long run, . . . • Because I value . . . , I think this side is heavier.
6. Clearly communicate why they chose one side over the other.	• We agreed that this side is heavier because the evidence of . . . scored higher on our criteria for what was important. • We disagreed at the end because I value . . . more and she values . . . more.

Table 3.1 Steps in the argumentation process and what students might say for these steps

To Disagree or Not to Disagree

Some of these activities can and do have sentence starters to support language uses. Remember to use these as needed, and to take them away as soon as possible. Also make sure they serve the purpose of building up ideas and evaluating evidence in an argument. For example, I have seen a lot of sentence frames that start with "I agree with you because…" and "I disagree with you because…" Usually, "I agree" is not as problematic as "I disagree." Yet, we must think about how agreeing and disagreeing, especially early on in the conversation, helps or not. Does it matter whether you agree with me when I share my idea (except for obviously wrong statements and facts)? No, it doesn't—what matters is that we find evidence to build up the idea. On the other hand, if you disagree right away, it might shut me down, and I might even stop listening. Instead of "I disagree," suggest to students that they just start saying their idea: "My idea is that…" Or they can say, "I have a different idea."

Activities for Improving Collaborative Argumentation

The following activities help build students' skills of objectively building more than one competing idea, evaluating the quality of evidence, comparing and choosing competing ideas, and explaining choices. Some are relatively unstructured activities, while others are more structured (i.e., not as back-and-forth or free-flowing) in order to (a) help students work on specific conversation skills and (b) provide structured face-to-face talk time for students who need to practice speaking and listening.

Pro-Con Improvisation

This activity helps students build speaking skills and sharpen their thinking about the pros and cons of a topic. It also trains them to use appropriate transitions and movements to communicate. It is low-prep, fun, and easily done in pairs. It becomes an effective foundational activity for many potential variations that you can use throughout the year as the complexity of subject matter increases.

1. Choose a student to be your partner for the modeling section of the activity. The student takes on the role of the director (the listener), while you model the role of the speaker. You are going to speak to both the pros and cons of a given topic in a series of turns. Tell the director that they need to listen to both sides every time in order to make a final decision on which side they think the speaker (you) leaned toward.

2. Choose a topic for the modeling. Typically, the speaker (i.e., you) picks the topic from a list of choices, but you can have the director choose (and surprise the speaker), or just give the class a topic that you have chosen.

3. After picking the topic, your director says, "Pro!" and claps. You make up the pro reasons for the topic for thirty seconds or so, and use any examples or evidence to strengthen the pro side. After a few sentences, the director claps and says, "Con!" and you immediately switch to the negatives of the topic, after starting the turn with an academic transition such as *however, on the other hand,* or *then again* (you are not allowed to use *but*). After describing a con, the director repeats the "Pro!" and "Con!" stages twice more. After you have completed all your turns, ask the director to tell you, "I think you leaned on the side of _____ because you _____."

4. Give the class a list of possible topics that lend themselves well to this activity. Here are a few common and easier topics to start with: camping, rain, shopping, movies, the beach, watching TV, dogs, parents, traveling, exercise, driving, social media, school, cars, and fast food. Eventually, you can give them meatier topics that pertain to your class, such as the Vietnam War, Thomas Jefferson, use of violence to fight for freedom, certain laws, technology, democracy, communism, nuclear power, Napoleon, the sun, and education.

5. Put students in pairs. They decide who will take which role for the first go. Encourage them to communicate the pro and con not only in their voices but also in body language and movement. The director should listen closely, with head nodding, eye contact, and posture showing engagement in the monologue.

6. Tell the directors to allocate fixed lengths of time for the talker to think and talk. This means that there might be slightly uncomfortable silences at times. Yet, these few seconds allow the talker to keep thinking. The director shouldn't "save" the talker by switching to pro or con after one sentence. For example, if a talker says, "Social media has a lot of bullying" and then is silent, the director should wait a few seconds, showing that he or she wants to hear more and that one sentence wasn't enough. If the talker still doesn't continue, the director can do one of three things: (1) prompt the speaker for clarification (*What kind of bullying?*), (2) prompt for support with examples or evidence (*Do you know of specific examples of bullying in social media?*), or (3) provide idea seeds that the talker can elaborate on to help him or her build up each side even more (*What about the suicides that connect to social media?*).

7. Stop the activity and ask the directors to tell their talkers, "I think you leaned on the side of _____ because you _____." Have students switch roles and switch topics.

8. Optionally, you can have them use the same topic, but give them different articles or information beforehand so that there is an information gap that they bridge with language. An added bonus is that they will build up both sides even more.

9. To finish, you can have students perform in front of the class and then have everyone discuss what they liked about the performances. What was strong about the communication on the part of the speaker? Did he or she smoothly transition from pro to con and back? You or they can also comment on good uses of academic language, prompts, and transitions.

Other variations of Pro-Con, which fall under the group of activities I call Transition Improv Activities, include For-Against (e.g., Using DNA to bring back dinosaurs. For! Against!), Similar-Different (e.g., Plant cells and animal cells. Similar! Different!), and Two Perspectives (e.g., Colonists!... Native Americans!), all of which have students flipping back and forth between opposing ideas and using transitions to do so.

Opinion Continuum

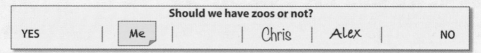

Figure 3.1 Example of an Opinion Continuum

This activity is a variation of the Stronger and Clearer activity that you saw in Chapter 2.

1. Ideally, have partners write their initial opinion (claim) down on paper. This can help to build confidence in what they will say initially. They turn this writing over and don't look at it until after the interactions with peers.

2. Have each student put their name on a sticky note, which they put on a continuum strip of paper that has the question in the middle and the opposing arguments on each side. Students should make the position of their sticky note on the strip reflect their own opinion on the question (See figure 3.1).

3. Put students into two facing lines, A and B.

4. Have line A students describe to their partners why they are located where they are on the continuum. Line B students should ask support and clarify questions to line A students (e.g., "Is there stronger evidence to support that idea?"). Remind students that one of their jobs is to help their fellow students strengthen and clarify their opinions.

5. Signal to change turns in a partnership—don't let them switch on their own, because they will tend to cut their times very short. Now line A listens and line B talks.

6. Once line B has finished, ask students to move their sticky notes if their opinion changed after the conversation. Have them give their reasons for moving (or not moving) to their partner.

7. Also have them tell each other, in ten seconds, what information or ideas they heard that they will use and share with future partners.

8. Then have them move so each student has a new partner. Now line B students share first. Before they start, remind them to use language and evidence (or respond to contrary evidence) from previous partners to make their opinions stronger and clearer this time. Remind them that having a stronger idea doesn't necessarily mean moving more toward the opposite sides of the continuum; it could mean going toward the center and having more and stronger reasons for being there.

9. After talking with and listening to three partners, have students write a postwrite response, without looking at the prewrite. Then they can see how the talking made a difference shaping their opinions. Some teachers have students highlight or underline in their postwriting the information that they got from others in their interactions.

Here is a sample transcript from an Opinion Continuum activity in fourth-grade English language arts, prompted by, *Should we have zoos or not?* Notice how A's answer gets stronger and clearer across the three turns because of the ideas gained from listening to others and from putting the thoughts into words three times. (T is the teacher.)

(1) A: I think zoos are fun. I like seeing animals. I say yes.

(2) B: I say no. It's like jail for them. And I don't like all the people looking at me.

(3) T: OK, move your opinion sticky, if needed, and tell your partner what ideas or evidence they gave that made you move, and any ideas that you will use with your next partner. And before you switch to a new partner, remember that your answer needs to be stronger and clearer than last time. OK, switch to new partners! This time, line B goes first.

(4) C: I think zoos are OK if the animals can't live wild. Last year I went to a zoo that helped hurt ones. Like an eagle with a broken wing. But other zoos are bad.

(5)   A: I was on yes but moved a little right. I don't wanna be in cages like animals. It's like jail. But I still think it's fun to go and see them. And like you said, some zoos help.

(6)   T: OK, move your opinion sticky, if your mind changed at all, and tell your partner what evidence or ideas of theirs made you move, and any ideas that you plan to use with your next partner. And remember that your answer should be the strongest and clearest ever, since it's your last chance. OK, switch!

(7)   A: I don't know. I moved it more to the middle each time. Animals don't like being in jail and people watching. And the cages are small. I think they get sad. But some get hurt and need people. Those zoos are good. Like they save eagles, maybe a broken wing. And we can learn from zoos, so yes.

Opinion Formation Cards

This activity is usually a pre-reading activity, but it can be altered for post-reading. Students use cards with quotations on them to build up their understandings of both sides of an issue, and then they make a more informed and more logical decision about where to stand on it.

> Cell phones make cheating much easier for students. They can take pictures of tests, text questions and answers, or even access notes and textbooks through their cell phones. Cell phones are so small these days, and students are so adept at using them surreptitiously that detecting their use is increasingly difficult.

Figure 3.2 Sample Opinion Formation Cards

> When I was teaching, all too often I turned around from writing something on the board to find students text-messaging or otherwise playing with their phones. Many students would fail the class and far too many would drop out of school due to the distractions in the classroom, the biggest being cell phones.

> The principal argued: "I don't know a businessperson, lawyer, or doctor out there who doesn't use a cell phone to learn and connect with others in professional ways. Why shouldn't students also learn to learn and communicate with them in schools?"

Figure 3.2 (continued) Sample Opinion Formation Cards

1. Choose evidence-laden quotations from one or more texts that support different sides of an issue, and put them on small cards or strips.

2. Tell students the issue and have them start forming their *own* opinion.

> With GoKnow's cell phone-based applications, a student could draw a concept map showing the relationship between water cycle processes, create an animation illustrating how it all looks, and write up a text report on what they've learned—all centralized on a desktop-like interface on the smartphone's screen.

3. Give students a card each. Have students read their card and think about how it supports, contradicts, or even changes their opinion. They do not have to take on the opinion supported by their card. But if it doesn't support their claim, they should prepare to address their quotation as counterevidence and explain why they don't think it is strong enough to persuade them to take that side. Optionally, they can first meet with a partner who has the same quotation to clarify its meaning and prepare a bit more.

4. Students then meet with other students who have different points (different quotations), read quotations to each other, and both state their current opinion on the issue. They can also ask questions and prompt for elaboration. Tell them that it's OK to change their opinions or how strongly they feel about a side as they talk to different partners. In fact, it's one of the goals.

5. After the activity, students write down their current opinion, with reasons and evidence.

6. Students read the article and see how their opinion changes through reading.

7. Optionally, they can have a final pair-share to share their final opinion and how it changed from the beginning of the activity.

Here is a sample conversation from sixth grade. The quotations were taken from an article on deforestation. The teacher had made three cards with quotations for deforestation and three cards with quotations against it. We follow student A's interactions.

(1)   A: My quote is, "Around half of deforested land is used for subsistence farming. This is usually done by a local family who cuts down trees to grow crops or raise livestock." Before this I thought we shouldn't cut any forests down. But some people need to grow food.

(2)   B: And they need wood, too.

(3)   A: Yeah. So I still think it's bad, but maybe they can just make it for families who live there.

(4)   B: OK, I have, "In the last 30 years, it is estimated that 90% of the rain forests in West Africa and South Asia have disappeared. In addition, 40% of the rain forests in Central America and 85% of the rain forests in Brazil have been cut down—that's an area twice the size of the state of Texas!" So this is a lot of forest, and that means it just becomes farmland or maybe just nothing there. So I think it's bad, but . . . even though it might help the families. Maybe they can do something else.

(5)   T: OK, switch partners! Remember to think about if you changed your opinion at all, and why. You can also say if your quotation supports your idea or not.

(6)   A: OK, I got, "Around half of deforested land is used for subsistence farming. This is usually done by a local family who cuts down trees to grow crops or raise livestock." This didn't support my idea cuz I thought we shouldn't cut down any trees, even though some families need to grow food to live. But also we gotta do something, because Alex's quote said like 90 percent of forests are gone.

(7)   C: Wow. That's bad. My quote is, "Logging companies provide jobs for millions of people who might not otherwise have consistent incomes. Local economies and governments in poor areas depend on the money that logging generates." So, millions of people is a lot, especially if they are poor. So I think logging is bad, but shouldn't be completely stopped cuz people might not be able to buy food.

(8)   T: OK, switch partners!

(9)   A: I got, "Around half of deforested land is used for subsistence farming. This is usually done by a local family who cuts down trees to grow crops or raise livestock." So I started off thinking no way, it should stop, and I still kinda think, that cuz 90 percent of forest is gone in lots of places. But I also think, I think families gotta live. And the trees help in poor places to make money, from logging, so people can buy food, you know? Maybe they let some families cut down a little and move on, and let some companies cut down some, but not all, like not cut down all the trees. Lots of animals live there.

(10) D: My quote is, "Plants in the rain forest defend themselves from insect predators by producing unique chemicals that are useful to people as medicines. It is estimated that 70% of the plants used to fight cancer are rain forest plants (National Cancer Institute). And only about 1 percent of the plants in rain forests have been studied for their medicinal prop- erties." So I think we should stop cutting them down, because we can maybe get medicines for diseases like cancer and other bad ones. And like you said, lots of forest is, are already gone, like cut down. But I also think we don't, we don't want people to be poor. They should have jobs. I don't know.

Notice the amplification and changes in student A's idea. This means that she was thinking about what she was hearing from others and from the texts. Also notice the use of texts as evidence and all the rich language that students used from the quotations to shape their ideas. Finally, think about how much more prepared for reading texts on this topic the students are as a result of this activity.

Modified Structured Academic Controversies

Structured academic controversies (SACs) (Johnson and Johnson 1994) are popular activities that focus on argument-based issues. With some adjustments, they can be powerful ways to build up students' conversational argumentation skills as described in this and the previous chapter. For example, you can modify an SAC in the following way:

- Choose an issue and craft the prompt so that it is engaging and has two or more sides to choose from. Students should feel like they have control (agency) over ideas and how they are built up. Students should suspend their opinions on the issue until the very end of the activity.

- Put students into teams of 6 to 8 to build up one of the sides of the issue together. Have them pair up to do initial research to then share with the team. They should also become familiar with the other sides and how to address evidence presented for them.

- Have a student in each team take notes on a building-ideas visual or use cards to build up ideas. This person can remind the team to clarify and support the terms and ideas that they are building up. Also have students discuss the quality of evidence gathered thus far and be prepared to share with another team.

- Then have two teams with different positions meet to come up with as much agreement as possible on which side is stronger (or heavier). They share their evidences with each other and what they see as strengths and weaknesses in the evidences and reasoning.

- Optionally, to avoid large discussion groups of 12 and 16 or more, you can have groups split up, put 3 or 4 members into the inner discussion circle and put the others in the outer circle. These outer circle members can take notes and support their inner circle members. Halfway through the discussion, inner and outer members switch to continue the discussion.

- At the end you can have students meet in pairs with a partner from a different group, and, without using notes, have a face-to-face conversation to finalize their decisions on the issue. They can also write their final ideas down.

You can increase the amount and quality of clarification and support during the team discussions by making sure that students work as hard as they can to build up and evaluate all ideas as well as they can. Use this and similar activities (e.g., debates) to explicitly analyze and apprentice students in the use of criteria, and to familiarize them with how people agree and differ with respect to using criteria to evaluate evidence within arguments.

Argument Balance Scale Conversations

This is a highly hands-on and minds-on activity that allows students to grasp, literally, the process of using criteria to weigh and compare two sides of an issue. There is a two-dimensional version, shown in Appendix B, but I recommend the three-dimensional version (Figure 3.4) that you can make from folded card stock. (Both are downloadable from this book's webpage on stenhouse.com.) The balance scale helps students build up both sides of an issue and then do some criteria-based comparing to decide which side is stronger. Issues from all content areas can be used. As you read the procedure and try this out, imagine students growing up into adults with the habits of building up all sides of an issue and then objectively using criteria to decide which is better. And imagine if more adults actually used this scale for their decisions.

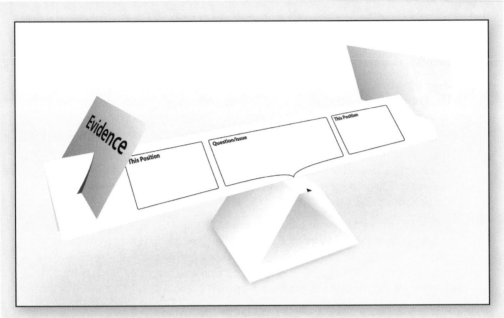

Figure 3.3 Argument Balance Scale Visual Organizer

Students work together to come up with reasons, evidence, and examples that support (give weight to) each side. Students should avoid stating their opinions at the beginning and instead wait until they have collaborated to fill in reasons and evidence on each side. You should model how to do the activity with a student. In the modeling you can show students that you want them to talk a lot as they set up the scale. You can model evaluation language such as *Which side weighs more? Why? Are any reasons bigger than other reasons? What criterion are you using? I think that this example is very strong because . . .*

Beforehand, show students how to cut out the pieces and put them together. You cut on the solid lines and fold on the dotted. The crossbar is an upside-down V when you put it on the trapezoid-shaped fulcrum that you tape together. The reason and evidence cards are different colors and are on opposite sides of the crossbar. They are also different sizes to represent their "weight," though some teachers I know use stickers or paper clips to represent weight. (Students get a certain number that they can attach to cards on each side.) Here is the procedure:

1. Each pair of students has a balance scale, and they both will build up both sides.

2. Students clarify the issue and write it in the center box. Then they clarify each side of the issue (or the top two competing claims, if there are several) to put in the side boxes.

3. Students start by brainstorming and gathering all the reasons and evidence for one side, putting them on a list next to that side. These include quotations, statistics,

anecdotes, and data. Emphasize to students that even though they might already lean toward a side in their minds, they should try to (a) not let the partner know it yet and (b) help build up both sides as much as possible (i.e., resist the temptation to withhold good information that might help build up the side you don't favor in your mind). Often students will change their minds after the conversation, and they can more easily do this if they didn't commit to a side early on.

4. Students collaborate to evaluate the strengths of the reasons and evidence on each side and choose the top three or four. They put the strongest reasons and evidence on the largest cards, and they should be able to explain their decisions. As students get older, they should try to be clearer in their use of criteria to evaluate and compare strengths and weights. This allows them to compare apples to apples, oranges to oranges, and bananas to bananas, so to speak. Students need to compare and prioritize criteria, a key skill within this skill. (See examples of criteria included at the beginning of this chapter.)

5. While building up both sides, students should poke holes in the reasons/evidence on the cards on each side, making them lighter, in a sense. The six arrows pushing up represent this. If one card says, *Pizza isn't healthy food*, a student might counter with, "But pizza has cheese, which has protein, tomato sauce, which is a vegetable and has vitamin C, and the dough is bread, which has carbohydrates that give the body energy." (I agree.) You can also allow students to cut off a corner or two of a card to represent weaknesses of the reason or evidence on it.

6. After building up both sides, students use criteria again to compare the sides and choose the heavier one. For example, a student may have cards on different sides with *High cost of incarceration* on one and *Rehabilitation programs are more effective* on the other. She may tell her partner that the cost of incarceration is too high and that the money could be used for other rehabilitation programs. Students can compare a card on one side with a card on the other, but they also need to compare the overall weights of each side to see which is heavier. At this point, because students will differ in what they value, they might disagree on which side is heavier. This is OK, as long as they can clearly describe their reasoning.

7. Students prepare to defend their choices orally. Then, optionally, they write an outline or rough draft of an article that explains their decisions and rationales.

Here is a sample conversation from fifth-grade history. The students had already filled in their balance scales before their conversations. The prompt was, *Imagine you are a woman in the colonial period. Should you stand up for women's equality and challenge the belief that women are inferior servants of men? Use the balance scale to make your decision. And use the present tense in first person. That is, use* I *and* we.

(1) A: So one evidence is that we are treated badly by men. There is violence on us all the time.

(2) B: That's a big one. It's wrong. And another one is that we can't be what we want to be in life. That's wrong, too.

(3) A: It's not fair.

(4) B: No. One more here is that men believe it because they are lazy, not just cuz of religion. I think they want us to be like slaves for them.

(5) A: OK, now the other side.

(6) B: The big one is that they call a woman a witch if they stand up. Like if I say I am the same as men, like equal, they call me a witch, and they kill me.

(7) A: That's crazy.

(8) B: Yeah. And they were religious, too. So, what's another one?

(9) A: I think some women believed it, you know. So if I'm one of those, I don't stand up or complain.

(10) B: But why would they believe that?

(11) A: I don't know. Like the teacher said, people were way different back then. Even now in lots of countries I think they still think it.

(12) B: Really? That's wrong. OK, other evidence for this side?

(13) A: No. So let's decide.

(14) B: OK. Well, the yes side has three and the no side has two.

(15) A: But this one about getting killed is pretty heavy.

(16) B: Yeah, but still. If they don't stand up/

(17) A: /We.

(18) B: We don't stand up, when does it end?

(19) A: Even if you die?

(20) B: Yeah. It's wrong. Maybe it'll help other women in the future if I die.

The balance scale helped to structure the conversation and keep them focused on building up both ideas. It was a little mechanical at times, but this type of practice will help these students in the future. And I also liked the dramatic aspect of having them take on the roles of women in that time period.

Take a Side and Convince Three on the Fence

You are likely familiar with the Take a Side activity, in which you pose a two-sided question and have students decide which side they will take and physically get up to be on that side of the room. In this variation, students on each side (you can also have three or four sides) try to persuade three fence-sitters to take one of the sides.

1. Come up with a controversial question based on a text or a topic the class is studying.

2. Have three students leave the room.

3. Have the other students choose a side of the issue and get up to stand on that side of the room.

4. Have students on each side pair up and share their reasons and evidence for choosing the side they chose. They should refer to the book, the text, and their own life. They should also talk about the evidence for the other side and why it is not as heavy as the side they have chosen.

5. Have each side huddle into a larger group and prepare arguments for persuading the three on the fence to come to their side.

6. Have the three fence-sitters come back in and sit in the middle of the room. Tell them the issue or question.

7. Flip a coin to decide which side goes first. Then call on three students from the side to say their reasons and evidence. Give about three to five minutes for this. The fence-sitters should ask clarifying questions and support questions such as "How does that evidence support your claim?"

8. Ask the other side if they want to challenge the value of the reasons and evidence that they just heard. Give this about a minute or so.

9. Then give the second side three to five minutes to share their reasons and evidence to persuade the fence-sitters to take their side.

10. Then allow the three students to decide where they want to be. They can stay in the middle, move partway over, or move all the way to a side. In any case, each needs to move and then share why they are in the spot they chose. They can say, "Even though the evidence supporting the _____ side was compelling, I thought the reasons and evidence for the _____ were heavier because . . ."

Here is a conversation excerpt from two sixth-grade bilingual students engaged in step 3. The teacher had given the prompt, *Should ancient tombs have their contents removed and put on display in a museum, and should the tombs then be open to the public?* These students had chosen to go to the yes side of the room. The students chose to converse in Spanish (See Table 3.2).

1.	A:	Pues, yo pienso que es importante aprender sobre ellos.	Well, I think that it's important to learn about them.
2.	B:	¿Por qué?	Why?
3.	A:	Porque no escribieron mucho y podemos aprender sus creencias y costumbres.	Because they didn't write much, and we can learn about their beliefs and customs.
4.	B:	Sí, pero el otro lado va a decir que no es justo molestar a los muertos.	Yes, but the other side will say that it isn't right to disturb the dead.
5.	A:	Pero podemos contestarles y decir que Howard Carter devolvió al rey Tut a su tumba.	But we can answer them by saying that Howard Carter returned King Tut to his tomb.
6.	B:	Y también podemos decir que la mayoría de las tumbas ya se habían saqueadas.	And we can say that the majority of the tombs had already been looted.
7.	A:	Otra razón sería para el turismo y el dinero que ganan en el país.	Another reason would be tourism and the money that the country earns.
8.	B:	Y también si las cosas de las tumbas están en el museo, es más difícil robarlas.	And also if the things from the tombs are in a museum, it's more difficult to steal them.
9.	A:	Y a lo major las personas pueden aprender más sobre las cosas en los museos.	And people can probably learn more about the things in museums.
10.	B:	El otro lado va a decir que los turistas hacen daño a las tumbas.	The other side will say that tourists harm the tombs.
11.	A:	¿Cómo?	How?
12.	B:	Con su aliento y las luces.	With their breath and the lights.
13.	A:	Pues, podemos decir que su dinero puede cobrar por reparar los daños.	Well, we can say that their money can pay for repairing the damages.
14.	B:	OK.	OK.

Table 3.2 Sample transcript (in Spanish) of a Take a Side activity

I chose this conversation to show how students can practice their conversation and argumentation skills in whatever language or languages they choose. Notice the turns in which students prepared to address counterevidence from the other side.

Court Case Simulation

Some of the most intense evaluating goes on in courtrooms. Cases with obvious verdicts seldom make it to court, since it would be a waste of time. Courts tend to decide our society's challenging issues and answer difficult questions that involve abstract dimensions and complicated laws. This activity, as you might guess, takes several days or more, so you must choose a meaty and high-mileage topic to make it worthwhile. If you choose well, though, you can get exceptional levels of analyzing, building, clarifying, supporting, comparing, and evaluating from your students.

1. Choose two similar issues that relate to what you are studying. You could choose one, but it is helpful to have the participants in one case be the jury for the other case, and vice versa, so that the jury's hearing of the case is more authentic (not informed by their own research on a case). Choose controversial and unclear cases that need to use criteria to stack up the evidence on each side. For example, the case may be about whether a crime was political, whether a medical practice is ethical, how evil a person is, and so on.

2. Discuss what a court case does and how criteria are used to make the decisions. Remind them that they must present the evidence in their favor in the hearing in the most persuasive and powerful way possible. They will need to practice their roles, but they will also need to be ready for unexpected situations.

3. Describe the order of the case. Draw the process on the board if needed.

   i.   Opening arguments

   ii. Questioning the witness(es) for the defense

   iii. Cross-examination of witness(es) by the prosecution

   iv. Questioning the witness(es) for the prosecution

   v.   Cross-examination of witness(es) by the defense

   vi. Closing arguments

4. Students read the background information needed to form their arguments, questions, and answers. They will form these notes around the central issue and the criteria. For example, three questions can help here: *Was it a political crime? What are the criteria for a political crime? How did this specific action fit the criteria?*

5. Model for students how to build a case for one side of an argument. There will be certain words and ideas that you will want to stick in the heads of the jury. Which questions and comments will do this? Have students order their notes from least to most powerful. Have them predict the questions that the other side will ask and the comments they will make. Prepare for counterarguments and for comments that can address them.

6. Optionally, you can design a graphic organizer, such as a chart or a web, that shows the strengths and weaknesses of the evidence. A chart might have six criteria down the left side and the two sides across the top. Students need to fill in how each side fits each criterion, if at all.

CRITERIA	EVIDENCE FOR	EVIDENCE AGAINST
(CRITERION 1)		
(CRITERION 2)		
(CRITERION 3)		
(CRITERION 4)		

Table 3.3 Criteria and evidence chart

7. Hold the simulation in the classroom or, ideally, in a more official room (e.g., district boardroom). Make it as "real" as possible. For example, the judge (most likely you) should use and model typical courtroom lingo: *This hearing is now in session . . . Defense, please call your first witness to the stand . . . In your closing argument, you mentioned that . . .*

8. During the simulation, scaffold all students' language and help to clarify points along the way. Help both sides as equally as possible.

9. When the process from step 3 is finished, the jury deliberates on the facts presented, with the help of the judge (i.e., you). Help them discuss the facts on both sides, and do not let them think you favor either side.

10. The jury returns. One member delivers the verdict and explains the rationale for their decision. You can clarify any points to bring closure to the activity. It is very helpful to have students reflect on the simulation and what they learned in the process. Even discussing feelings of like and dislike, with reasons, are helpful.

11. Optionally, have students write a paragraph or two—perhaps you can call it a newspaper article—that describes the proceedings, the decision, and the reason for the decision. All students should understand both cases and the arguments for both.

Conclusion

As you likely saw in this chapter, collaborative argumentation is different from what many students think argumentation is. As students think less about winning in a conversation, they can think more about building up ideas, applying criteria, and making objective decisions. And this set of skills, of course, will help them well beyond the school walls. I also hope that you have a stronger sense of collaborative argumentation's potential for the development of content, thinking, and language.

For additional suggestions and research on collaborative argumentation, see works by Felton et al. (2015), Chinn and Clark (2013), and Osborne (2010).

Chapter 4

Conversations Across Disciplines

*True connectedness is
face-to-face conversation.*

W hile the skills in the previous chapters are found in most academic conversations, this chapter highlights key differences between conversations in the disciplines of English language arts (ELA), English language development (ELD), math, science, history, and social studies. The most significant differences are the thinking skills used, the products of the conversations (ideas built up or decided), the prompts that shape the conversations, and the lesson designs that both support and are supported by conversations. This chapter provides examples of prompts, conversations, activities, and lesson plans in different content areas.

Conversations in English Language Arts

English and language arts classes cover a lot of ground. Students in these classes must first learn how to use language, which means using language to get things done. They must also learn how language works, which includes grammar and organization of ideas. They must learn to write, which in school is usually expository and requires a heavy dose of evidence to support ideas. Finally, they must improve their reading of a wide range of nonfiction and fiction texts each year, which includes comprehension skills such as interpreting, making inferences, using literary devices, supporting ideas, and so on. Conversation activities can help students tackle multiple skills at once, embed them in real-world interactions, and make learning last.

There are different "types" of conversations in ELA settings. I include three fairly big and broad ones: (1) conversing to comprehend nonfiction texts, (2) conversing to improve writing, and (3) conversing to interpret literature. I chose these because of their potential to make a big difference in the development of students' language and reading abilities.

ELA Type 1—Conversing to Comprehend Nonfiction Texts

Perhaps more now than ever before, students need to be good readers of nonfiction texts. Even though they might, at times, need to comprehend texts that don't have sentences (e.g., images, directions, manuals, advertisements), here I focus on sentence-based nonfiction texts that students typically encounter at school, such as textbook chapters, articles, essays, biographies, and other expository pieces.

Figure 4.1 gives a working model of comprehension, which may always be in draft form. Despite the wide variations in how students read (and the widely varying models of comprehension), it can help to take a look at models like this one, even if it is just to see where they fall short. The central dimension is the essence of comprehension: constructing new and clearer meaning that matches the author's and comprehender's purposes.

All five dimensions work together, with thoughts bouncing between them at lightning speed, to build up an understanding of the text. As the reader puts the words and sentences together, she also uses her background knowledge to visualize the meanings of words and sentences and connect them to any other related knowledge. All the while she keeps track of how well the meanings are matching the central purposes for reading or listening. At the same time, the student uses comprehension strategies such as making inferences and asking questions, in concert with thinking skills such as interpretation and empathy, to further solidify and clarify the meaning of the message. Yes, there's a lot going on in a reader's head when comprehending a text.

In looking at this model in Figure 4.1, notice how much there is to talk about in conversations about a text. Another person comprehends differently and can offer new insights, questions, answers, descriptions, and arguments. When two students talk about a text, they amplify its potential. Students, roughly speaking, have over a dozen different things to talk about in their conversations about texts. And a huge added bonus is that every student will use these dimensions in different ways to comprehend the same text. This means that they have plenty of unique perspectives to share with others. But, as you can imagine, you can't just put this model up on a poster and say, "Go!" It's a lot of work to get students to the point of having long and rich comprehension-focused conversations.

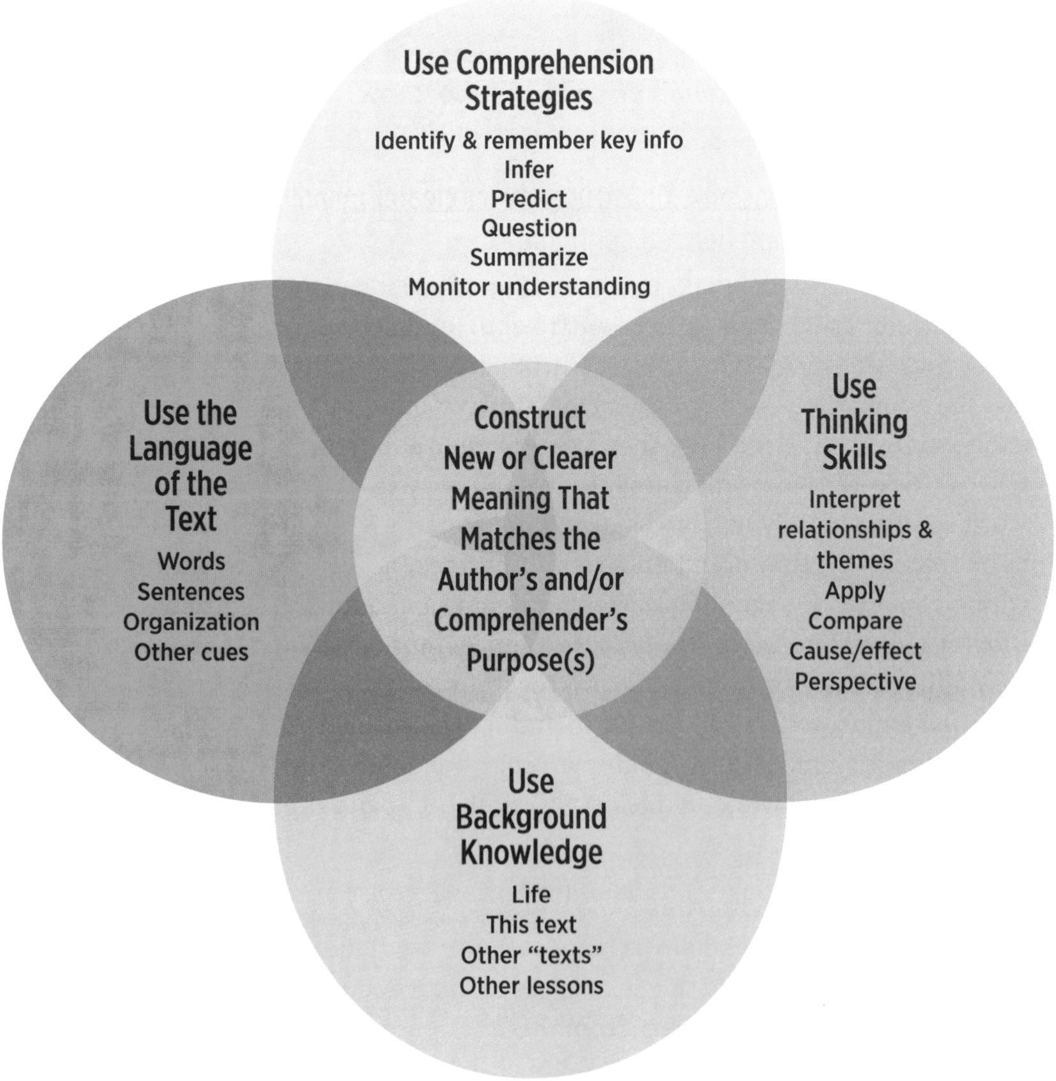

Use Comprehension Strategies

Identify & remember key info
Infer
Predict
Question
Summarize
Monitor understanding

Use the Language of the Text

Words
Sentences
Organization
Other cues

Construct New or Clearer Meaning That Matches the Author's and/or Comprehender's Purpose(s)

Use Thinking Skills

Interpret relationships & themes
Apply
Compare
Cause/effect
Perspective

Use Background Knowledge

Life
This text
Other "texts"
Other lessons

Figure 4.1 A basic model of how comprehension works

So, in this section, I describe the five dimensions in the model, each with several suggestions and sample prompts for helping students hold *comprehension conversations* about nonfiction texts. They talk to sharpen their own and their partners' abilities to understand a wide range of texts. It is a bit longer than other sections because of its complexity. I will refer to it in the descriptions of other content areas later in the chapter, and I will show how these dimensions are used to interpret literature later in the third type of ELA conversation.

Comprehension Dimension 1: Construct new or clearer meaning that matches the author's and comprehender's purpose

In conversation, students co-construct (co-build) ideas that the text was meant to help them build. This is the central skill, and good readers need to use the other four skills to perform this central skill. The challenge is to manage and use the appropriate skills at the right times to build up the ideas as effectively as possible. During reading, they need to monitor their understanding to see when it is weak and needs fixing up in some way (e.g., rereading, figuring out a word, looking closely at the visual, asking someone). Many students, however, don't realize that they aren't understanding a text as well as they need to. That's where conversation can help. Often students (and adults) need to try out their evolving ideas on others to compare their comprehensions. If their ideas are very different, the partners can work together to figure out why. Over time, this repeated exposure to how others, including the teacher, comprehend complex texts helps students improve their own comprehension and monitoring skills.

To help students work on this central skill, they can ask each other questions:

- Why did the author write this?
- Why are we reading this?
- How does this text help us build up our idea that ____?
- What new ideas did this text get us to think about building?
- What do we need to learn from this?
- Are we understanding this? What else do we need to understand this better?

Granted, the purpose for reading and conversing matters. If the reading is meaning and learning focused, then the conversation has a chance. If the reading and its conversation are just focused on answering non-interesting comprehension questions for points, then the conversation likely will be weak.

The more you have engaging topics, texts, and purposes for reading them, the more your students will engage in meaningful conversations.

Comprehension Dimension 2: Use the language of the text

Most conversations about the text will be after students have read at least a part of it. I know that many of you do have before-reading "text walk" conversations in which you preview the text, its headings, and its visuals to predict what ideas will be in it. But more often, students will talk about what they have read. Encourage students to take notes, to look at challenging words and sentences, and to bring them up in conversation. Have them talk about idiomatic expressions, why the author included or excluded certain effects, loaded language, and so forth. Here are a few questions that students might ask each other:

- Why did the author use this word (sentence, paragraph, visual)?
- How is this text/message organized? Why?
- What words or other clues show us which thinking skills to use for this text?
- What are the key words in this text? Why?
- What does this long sentence mean?

Comprehension Dimension 3: Use comprehension strategies

Most lists of comprehension strategies include identifying key information, summarizing, questioning, predicting, and making inferences. (There are others on these lists, such as connecting to background knowledge and figuring out unknown words, that I put into other dimensions in the model.) Imagine trying to read without these strategies. If you can't summarize long sentences, paragraphs, and larger portions of text, you can't fit them into your brain and remember them. If you don't remember what was written on the last page in an article on bears, for example, you can't build up what the current page is describing. If you don't fill in the blanks with inferences or predictions, and then see whether they are right as you read on, comprehension suffers. And if you don't ask questions, your brain doesn't look for answers in the text or elsewhere, and you don't understand as much. Getting students to model for and prompt each other to use these strategies a lot can improve students' overall comprehension abilities.

Here are a few questions that students might ask each other to help them use comprehension strategies more effectively:

- How is ___ important?
- Can you summarize what we read so far?
- Can you summarize this paragraph?
- Why do you think ... did (or said) that? (inference)
- What do you think the author will include in the next section?
- I have a question ...
- Do you have a question?

Comprehension Dimension 4: Use thinking skills

Readers need to use thinking skills to comprehend academic texts. Most nonfiction texts tend to structure ideas in one or more of these different ways: compare/contrast, cause/effect, taking other perspectives, argumentation, and application of ideas to life. If we can get students to push one another to use thinking skills each time they talk about texts, they will read better.

Here are a few questions that students might ask each other to help them use thinking skills more effectively:

- What is a strong theme or argument in this text?
- What does this evidence/data mean?
- How strong is the evidence for ... ?
- How are these connected?
- How are ... and ... similar/different?
- What is his/her perspective on ... ?
- How can we apply these ideas to life?

Comprehension Dimension 5: Use background knowledge

Even before you start reading a text, you use the existing cues (visuals, title, headings, etc.) to connect to what you already know about the topic to the text so you can start building up ideas. Often you visualize images or relationships based on what the text says and what you have in your head. Of course, the more background knowledge on a topic you have, the more likely you will understand a text on that topic. But even when you don't have a lot of background knowledge, you have learned to make connections to, and meaning out of, even semi-related knowledge. Students can benefit in three ways from conversations with peers that involve background knowledge about texts. They can (a) get more background knowledge from partners, (b) bring up and clarify their own knowledge related to the topic and see what the partner thinks of his or her connections, and (c) see how others make connections to, and use of, related knowledge.

Here are some questions they can ask one another:

- Can you connect this to any previous texts, problems, or events in your life?
- Is there a current idea in your head that this text helps to build (or challenge) in any way?
- What are you visualizing when you read this portion of text?
- How do the text and your experience help you predict or infer that?

As you have probably noticed by now, this section promotes getting students to prompt each other for things that teachers often prompt for. Imagine if you could split into thirty versions of yourself and meet one-on-one with all of your students at the same time. That's the power of peers asking each other teacherly comprehension-focused questions to build ideas in their conversations.

Sample Comprehension Conversation Excerpt

These students (both English learners) had just read a short article on the effects of the pesticide DDT on the food web in Kalimantan, Indonesia. The teacher instructed students: "Ask each other at least one question from each of the dimensions in our comprehension model in order to figure out and build up the main idea. If you hear a short answer, try to get your partner to clarify it or support it from the text."

(1)	A:	Why did the author write this?
(2)	B:	Maybe to show problems of DDT.
(3)	A:	What problems?
(4)	B:	They want to kill mosquitoes. For malaria. But they killed other things and it was . . . *peor* (worse).
(5)	A:	And maybe show problems of a food web. So they don't do it again. OK, you ask.
(6)	B:	Language. What does it mean, "When one part of the web, or even one organism, is disturbed, it can cause an undesired chain reaction?"
(7)	A:	I do *disturb* and you do *chain reaction*. (*They look up* disturbed *and* chain reaction.) *Disturb* means change, *cambiar*. So the food chain . . . changes.
(8)	B:	*Chain reaction* is a "series of events that cause one another." It's what happened. The lizards ate cockroaches. Cats ate lizards. Cats died and rats come in.

(9) A: Yeah. OK, a thinking question. What's evidence to support the main idea?

(10) B: I think this chain reaction. Like you said, is very bad. People die. OK, you do a comprehend question.

(11) A: Why the people die?

(12) B: They got sick. From rats, or from bugs in rats. Fleas.

(13) A: *Y es peor que la malaria* (and it's worse than the malaria).

(14) B: Yeah.

As you can see, even though this conversation isn't as natural as others in this book, using the questions from different comprehension dimensions can help extend the conversation and foster comprehension skills and strategies. You can play around with how you structure these. Just make sure to emphasize that students should prompt and respond to prompts for the purposes of understanding, not for points or for making you happy.

ELA Type 2—Conversing to Improve Writing

Academic conversations can provide students with rich practice using language orally before using it in writing. When students converse before they write, they get to practice using the language that they might use in their compositions and see how well partners understand what they are trying to say. And they often hear new language from others that they also can use. Even during the drafting, editing, and revising stages, conversations help students analyze the clarity of language used, especially when partners provide feedback. After writing, conversations help students to work on their ideas even more and practice orally with the more academic uses of language that they just used in their writing. Most strategies for teaching writing can be augmented with conversations in some way. Here are a few suggestions.

Modified Writing Process

The writing process tends to include the stages in Table 4.1. Most of the stages can benefit from short or long conversations with some extra modeling and guidance from the teacher. One of the most important features is the hardest to foster: motivation to communicate. It takes a lot of effort to write (e.g., even now my brain is stressing over what to write next). And if it's worth it, not just for points but to actually inform someone of something important or to change someone's mind about an important topic, then the motivation might be enough. The conversations can support the stages, and the stages can support conversations and their skills. Remember, building up ideas in conversation transfers well into building up ideas on paper.

Prompts should be crafted to initiate the building of original ideas, to use target vocabulary, and to experiment with new grammar. Teachers scaffold these academic conversations by modeling the language, offering response starters, and providing word banks.

STAGE	HOW TO FORTIFY IT CONVERSATIONALLY
1. Brainstorm what to write about (whole class or in small groups or pairs). This often happens after reading or watching a text. Choose one idea.	Pair students and have them prompt each other for ideas. Then they narrow them down and talk about which one is better to write about, and why.
2. Gather information that might be needed to write about the idea. Organize it.	Students can converse about how to fill in any holes or ways to strengthen their writing. They can also talk about how they will organize the information or argument (e.g., semantic map, T-chart, Argument Balance Scale).
3. Write the initial rough draft.	After drafting, pairs do a text walk through their own writings. They start with one piece and look at each sentence and co-decide whether it is complete and clear enough. They take turns reading the drafts out loud to one another. Partners ask questions such as "What idea are you building? Is that the strongest evidence? How does it support your main claim? Can you add some sentences to clarify what you mean by . . . ?"
4. Revise the writing (using the feedback of teacher, peers, others) to make it as strong and as clear as possible.	Pairs split up and students find new partners who read their drafts. The new partner talks about whether and how to organize, add, or subtract ideas, and whether to change the language to improve the clarity (e.g., use more details, use more precise terms).
5. Edit for grammar and punctuation.	Both students read their drafts to one another and talk about where and if punctuation or grammar changes are needed. If a piece of language sounds weird, they should talk about how to make it sound better.
6. Write final draft and publish.	Before writing the final draft, students can read their own drafts aloud, or listen to partners reading them, and make any suggestions for the final version.

Table 4.1 Ways to strengthen writing process stages with conversation

Here is a conversation excerpt from two seventh-grade students in a sheltered English classroom having a conversation about character changes at the first stage of writing workshop. The writing prompt was, *How did Esperanza change throughout the novel* (Esperanza Rising)? *Write three paragraphs on how she changed and if those changes made her a better person. Make sure to give and get as much evidence as you can when you talk.* The graphic organizer they had completed before the discussion had three rows to take notes about a character's changes. The organizer had three columns: one for the change, one for evidence in the beginning of the story, and one for evidence from the end of the story. Each row was for a different type of change (e.g., rich to poor, arrogant to humble, not knowing about the world to knowing more).

(1)   A: So how's she change?

(2)   B: She's rich in Mexico and poor in California.

(3)   A: I got that, too.

(4)   B: What other change you got?

(5)   A: I got she was selfish, like *egoísta*, in Mexico. Then not selfish, nice, at the end.

(6)   B: What's evidence?

(7)   A: For beginning, it, here, she doesn't let the little girl touch her doll. On the train. It was mean, cuz she's *consentida* (spoiled).

(8)   B: What about the end?

(9)   A: She gives the doll to a little girl. That's not selfish.

(10) B: I didn't have that *[takes notes]*. OK, I got lazy to hard worker.

(11) A: Evidence?

(12) B: Miguel teached her how, *como se dice, barrer*?

(13) A: Sweep.

(14) B: Sweep! She doesn't know how to sweep! Can you believe that? But later she works hard for money cuz her mom is sick.

(15) A: Yeah *[taking notes]*. That's important cuz you gotta work hard in life.

Here are some helpful writing-centered questions that I often ask teachers about student conversations like this: *What strengths and needs do you notice in the conversation between these two students? What were they able to do language-wise (vocabulary, sentences, organization)? How did they use conversation skills to improve their conversation? How might this conversation support their writing on the topic? If you were their teacher, what might you work on next to move them forward to improve their writing?*

Describe and Narrate Information Gap

In this activity, each student in a pair reads different texts or cards or looks at different visuals. You can do this in pairs, or you can do it with three or four in a group. Initially, they shouldn't look at the information of others.

1. Give each student some text(s) or images to look at. For example, a teacher might give all the A's in pairs the same text or set of pictures, and all the B's would get a different text or set of pictures.

2. Each student takes some time to look at his or her text or images.

3. Each student then explains, without showing it, one resource. For example, you might give each student a picture of different characters, with a description of their personalities, flaws, and desires. Each student practices, orally, describing to the partner the character, along with the image's background, without reading off the picture.

4. Next, each student does the same with any other pictures or text (settings, events, etc.).

5. The students converse to create a narration that connects all of the pictures or texts into some form of story or sequence.

6. Optionally, students can then join up with another pair to share ideas and create a group story.

ELA Type 3—Conversing to Interpret Literature

When it comes to literature (e.g., novels, stories, songs, poems), students can understand and interpret the same work in very different ways. These initial interpretations are raw materials for a variety of ways to build ideas in conversation. Several helpful thinking skills support and deepen conversations about literature. I focus on the skill of interpreting in this section. Additional skills and information related to collaborative interpreting can be found in resources such as book clubs (Raphael, Florio-Ruane, and George 2001), literature circles (Daniels 2002), Socratic seminars (Moeller and Moeller 2001), and reading workshop (Fountas and Pinnell 2001). These approaches have helped many students to converse about literature in deeper ways.

Interpreting literature helps readers to better understand what it means to be human. Literature offers readers brief windows into the minds and experiences of other people, present and past, near and far, to learn how they lived and thought about life. In my own classroom, I kept a permanent poster on the wall with all the themes that came up in the literature we had read. It kept growing over the years, and I am still building many of those themes in my mind as I read texts, even today.

Interpreting involves combining text information with related background knowledge to generate meanings (e.g., themes) that the author likely intended but did not directly tell us. Often a theme will come from looking at events and character actions, words, or changes (physical, psychological, etc.). Ideas about themes often differ across students, and even the same student might see different themes when reading the same story at different points in time. The most important themes tend to solidify when readers construct them on their own, usually connecting the themes to their own lives. In a nutshell, we want students to build up meaningful themes and ideas in a text without getting too far out on a tangent. This isn't always easy. In a sense, we want students to dig into and underneath the text, but we don't want them to tunnel miles away from the text and into a dead end. A good mantra that reminds students to build up ideas is, *Figuring out themes should not be the goal—it should be to build up themes and argue why they are important in life.*

An important skill that strengthens interpretation is empathizing and seeing other perspectives. Readers understand more when they empathize with characters, seeing the world through the eyes and hearts of others, including characters in stories, authors, literature experts, and other readers. Taking different perspectives tends to get students more engaged in a story and think about what they might do in similar situations. And all this can be clarified and built up in conversations, especially as one advantage of conversation with others is that you get to see how others think and feel. As a result of talking about characters in stories, partners can jointly build their understandings of characters and connect works of literature to life.

Here is a sample conversation from two ninth graders who were reading *Fahrenheit 451*. The prompt was, *At this point in the novel, what do you think the author's purpose was for writing it? To help you build this idea, try to use at least one prompt from each dimension on the chart [see Figure 4.1]. Remember, if you ask a question or say a prompt, it should help you and your partner build up an idea.*

(1)   A: OK, so from the middle one, "What do we need to learn from this?"

(2)   B: I think it's a way to scare us about the future, like how bad it can get. What about you?

(3)   A: Wait, so how does it, is it meant to scare us?

(4)   B: Well, with the fires and going into homes and burning books. If the government gets like that, it could happen. They could/

(5)   A: /And the TV walls, too. Maybe he's warning us about TV and what it does to our brains.

(6)   B: OK, this oval. Why do you think the bad guy, the boss, said, "If you don't want a house built, hide the nails and wood. If you don't want a man unhappy politically, don't give him two sides to a question to worry him" and "Give the people contests they win by remembering the words to more popular songs or the names of state capitals or how much corn Iowa grew last year. Cram them full of noncombustible data, so full of 'facts' they feel stuffed, but absolutely 'brilliant' with information."

(7)   A: I think it's the government. It wants to keep people too busy to think about important things/

(8)   B: /Or to criticize the government, right?

(9)   A: Yeah. They hide the nails and wood, which maybe means they don't tell you what is going on, or they lie. What's *noncombustible*?

(10) B: Here *[looks it up]*, it means it doesn't burn. So like I think noncombustible data is just stuff that isn't important or maybe, it's like not the stuff they like to burn when they go into houses.

(11) A: Or need to burn.

(12) B: Yeah, so thinking skills. How do we apply this?

(13) A: I think government still does this.

(14) B: Really?

(15) A: Uh-huh. Listen to what that White House person says. They never say anything bad about what they do. And they distract from really bad things they say or do.

(16) B: I agree.

(17) A: But what about burning books?

(18) B: Some schools ban books from libraries, but that's not the government.

Like the conversation in ELA Type 1, you likely noticed that this was not a free-flowing conversation, but I also hope you saw the advantages of having students respond to prompts from each dimension of the comprehension model. Conversations are much better when students work to develop a deep understanding of the texts they are reading.

Socratic Conversations

Socratic seminars, discussions, and circles are conversations that tap into the power of conversation for exploring, questioning, building, challenging, and negotiating ideas. Usually grounded in the use of questions, these conversations spark, foster, and extend ideas. Questions should focus on identifying symbols, metaphors, motives, themes, techniques, and author styles, along with any underlying meanings in character actions and words. Students should walk away from the conversations with good questions, new ideas, and a desire to engage in further conversations about the topics. As much as possible, try to have students run the conversations and not depend on you to come up with the guiding questions.

During a Socratic conversation, a group of students uses questions and answers to critique the consistency and logic of an idea and to clarify definitions of key terms. For example, if a student says: "I think we will learn more and better without grades," other students might prompt the group to clarify what *learn* and *grades* mean. Further questions might ask for examples and even challenge the logic of the cause-and-effect relationship in the statement. Answers and questions are usually followed by more questions. Eventually, a clearer or even a contrary theme might develop, such as "In many cases the extrinsic rewards of grades are not sufficient for lasting learning . . . " or "Many students and parents need to see the numbers that count up what we are learning. And some students are motivated by grades but not by other things . . . "

Here is a typical procedure for this kind of discussion, with modifications based on the ideas in this book:

1. Begin the conversation with a big question or controversial statement of truth. (Socrates focused on abstract concepts such as wisdom, courage, morality, truth, and justice.) The idea can come from students, often in response to what they are reading. I often suggest that students work toward a final idea, or "product," that will come from the conversation. Yes, the engaging nature of the topic is often enough for most students, but the extra incentive of "I can use these ideas beyond this conversation" tends to help.

2. Have pairs or small groups engage in practice Socratic conversations before the larger group discussions. This allows them to form and respond to questions as they practice creating and challenging ideas in a smaller setting. Highlight the importance of asking clarification, support, and evaluation questions to build up ideas (as you have seen aplenty already in this book). They can also practice with the Idea-Building Cards or Idea-Building Visual described in Chapter 2. I often tell teachers to try to get as much as they can out of the pair time, since it is lower stress and so more language happens then.

3. For the larger group discussion, put half the class in an inner conversation circle and the other half in an outer circle. Have each outer-circle student align themselves to be a copilot partner with one inner-circle student. Allow students some time in these inner-outer pairs to prepare their initial statements or questions.

4. Then have the whole group start discussing. The inner-circle students should try to clarify, expand, challenge, and uncover beliefs, truths, and opinions. But, as we saw in Chapter 3, students should build up the initial idea posed before challenging it. They shouldn't quickly shut down a potentially buildable idea.

5. While the discussion happens, outer-circle copilots listen and note down things they think could go into the discussion (e.g., clarifying questions). They can pass these notes to their partners. At certain points you can have partner breaks, in which the copilots provide suggestions to their partners when they turn back around to contribute to the group discussion.

6. Inner and outer circles then switch. If the topic still has some building to go, the new inner circle can continue building it up. Or the new inner circle can work on building up another topic.

7. You can conclude the activity by putting students into pairs and groups of four to serve different purposes. In a *pair-to-square* structure, pairs have a conversation that prepares them to converse with another pair. In a *square-to-pair*, groups of four start off a conversation before partners finish processing the ideas in pairs. In *mini-fishbowls*, one pair observes another pair in conversation and provides feedback afterward, and then they switch.

Role-Based Improvisation Conversations

This activity allows students to assume a character role in order to describe that character's perspectives, values, motives, and feelings. In particular, it gives reticent students a creative way to express themselves and verbalize ideas. The activity is inventive, academic, and fun. It can also lead to some interesting writing. Here is the procedure:

1. Pick a story or poem whose characters have different thoughts (perspectives, opinions, backgrounds, values, goals, etc.) that students could share with one another.

2. Craft a prompt that gets students to take on character roles and share their perspectives (e.g., take on the role of the mother and the son, share your character's perspective in first person, talk like the person would, try to decide what to do about the new dog that the son brought home).

3. Assign roles for each pair (e.g., mother and son).

4. Have students read the text with the prompt and their character in mind, taking notes on what they might say.

5. Have students go over their notes and synthesize the most important points onto one note card, using key words—not complete sentences.

6. With the prompt and their roles in mind, students converse (using conversation skills, etc.).

English Language Development

Many of you also teach some type of English language development (ELD) during a dedicated time during the school day. Some of you do this all day and some of you use a pull-out, push-in, or other co-teaching model. Whatever the case, here is a powerful, if not radical objective: *Don't teach language to teach language; instead, teach something interesting and support the language for doing so.* This approach doesn't sit well with many published ELD and ESL (English as a second language) textbooks and resources. These tend to be filled with a smorgasbord of texts and pages packed with grammar and vocabulary exercises to fill up an entire year (and more). Yet, as you might have gathered by now, I strongly argue for *authentic* use of language, even if it's messy and imperfect, to get interesting things done and to build engaging ideas in the minds of students.

I am often asked whether students at beginning levels of proficiency in English (or whatever target language) can or should be engaging in conversation. *They better be!* is the first response that comes to my mind. The conversations tend to have fewer spoken words and sentences, but when conversations are effectively supported, students can still build up engaging grade-level ideas. Support can be linguistic support (modeling and sentence starters), extra practice (as in Stronger and Clearer Each Time and Information Gap activities), conversation models, and visual models of idea-building. All of these are described in this and other chapters.

To increase authenticity in ELD conversations, we need to think about which topics interest students and design tasks around those topics. When I am asked for recommendations, I often suggest looking for or creating curriculum that focuses on one engaging area for at least a quarter, or ideally, a semester or more. For example, for several districts I suggested a semester of science-based ELD and a semester of history-based ELD. Often the topics had some engaging questions or controversies that kept students interested and pushed them to think and talk, much more than they would have by doing exercises or memorizing dialogues for points or praise.

Right from the start, students need to know that their ideas about content and language are highly valued by teachers and other students, even though their abilities to describe all of their rich thoughts are not yet fluent. Consider the following conversation in seventh grade, prompted by *Do trees talk?* after watching a video and having a class discussion on the topic. The teacher had just modeled in a conversation how to prompt for clarification with *Why?* and how to prompt for support with *Can you give an example?*

(1)	A:	Do trees talk?
(2)	B:	No.
(3)	A:	Why?
(4)	B:	No mouth. No words.
(5)	A:	But trees say. *Se comunican.* (They communicate with each other.)
(6)	B:	How?
(7)	A:	Chem . . . chemicals.
(8)	B:	Example?
(9)	A:	Bugs go eat the tree *[pointing to picture]*. Tree give chemical in air. Other trees ready.
(10)	B:	Ready? What's it mean?
(11)	A:	*Listo para defenderse contra los insectos.* (Ready to defend themselves against insects.)
(12)	B:	OK. Like talk, but not, not words. Use chemicals help others.
(13)	A:	Yes.

Notice the building of a robust idea with different language than proficient speakers would use. Notice the use of their first language at times to help clarify ideas. And consider all the engaged thinking, listening, and speaking that happens even in this short conversation.

Conversations in Math

Three very persistent myths hinder deep learning in math: (1) you need to solve problems quickly, (2) mistakes are bad, and (3) you need to work individually. Take a moment to think about why these myths can harm students' learning of math, and how conversations might be able to reduce this harm. Conversations in math allow students to

- take more time to think about problems and different ways to solve them;
- realize their own mistakes and learn from them;
- learn from the ideas and mistakes of others and
- work with peers to clarify and justify ideas.

And yet, as you know, productive conversations don't tend to just happen when you put students together and tell them to work together to solve a problem. It takes quite a bit of effort to go beyond the all-too-common scenario in which the more proficient math student in the pair or group solves the problem and lets the others copy his or her work. Productive conversations can help us shift the emphasis from merely getting the right answer to understanding the math behind the problem, using multiple methods to solve it, and communicating one's thinking to others. Finding the right answer should be just one part of what students focus on and do.

Most of the latest lists of standards place more emphasis than before on communicating mathematical thinking to others. As students listen and respond to their peers, they tend to clarify their own thinking, confusions, and misconceptions. And they can help others. Teachers also can learn a lot about student strengths and misconceptions during conversations.

As you remember from Chapter 2, building big ideas is vital to learning in deep and lasting ways. This is doubly true for math. Yet many students enter math class thinking, "How many problems do I have to do today for points?" Most students are not thinking, "What key mathematical ideas and skills am I building, and how will the problems I solve today help me do this building?" And yet, this is what we should want and what we need to foster. Conversations can help.

Here are three different types of conversation in math that can help students build ideas and help you to see their learning along the way: (1) collaborating to solve a problem, (2) collaborating to create new math problems, and (3) collaborating to explore, experiment with, and express mathematical concepts.

Math Type 1: Collaborating to solve a problem

Students should learn how to work together to solve problems. But, as I said above, it is vital to foster conversation that is focused on more than how quickly they can get the answer. In productive math conversations, students share their ideas and, more important, their reasoning and justification for the procedures they use. They also need to feel safe and valued even when their ideas are critiqued by others. One way to shape and deepen their math conversations is to use the Math Paired Conversation Protocol. Here are the steps and a sample conversation from sixth grade on ratios (see Table 4.2).

The problem: *Mr. S loves chocolate-covered raisins. He likes the small packets but wants to know if he should buy a big container of them instead to save money. Help him out and let him know how much he might save. The 8-ounce packets cost $1.50 apiece and the large 128-ounce container is $20.00.* The teacher said, "Follow the protocol and come up with a final idea that this problem is supposed to help you learn. And I would like you to use the term *unit price* in your final presentation."

MATH PAIRED CONVERSATION PROTOCOL (WHAT STUDENTS DO)	CONVERSATION EXAMPLE
Individually, look at the problem, estimate the answer, and think about possible ways to solve it.	(A and B read the problem and think about it.)
Work together to clarify what the problem says and what it is asking. Students should make sure that they understand any new or strange terms, along with what "happens."	A: I think we gotta figure out what costs more so we can tell Mr. S. B: I agree. But what's a protocol? A: I think it's the directions; this whole thing.
Share their estimates for the answer and justify the estimate.	B: What's your estimate and why? A: I think the bigger one. Cuz usually that's less money. B: OK. That makes sense. So what should we do?
Brainstorm ways to begin solving the problem, don't criticize the ideas, and decide to use at least two possible methods.	A: Maybe use a double number line cuz we did those this week. B: OK. And maybe another is divide them. I don't know which to divide. But we can start with the number lines. I like those.

Table 4.2 Math Paired Conversation Protocol with a sample conversation

MATH PAIRED CONVERSATION PROTOCOL (WHAT STUDENTS DO)	CONVERSATION EXAMPLE
Choose a method; one student "leads" (draws or writes) as the other helps and keeps asking, *Why?*—even if he or she knows why. This fosters verbalization of ideas and justifications.	A: OK, I'll start *[draws two parallel lines]*. I put . . . I think I put the 8 on one line and the $1.50 on the other. Like even with each. B: Why? A: Cuz they go with each other. It's a ratio. The 132 and 20. B: Make sure the 20 is on the money line. A: OK. Then I make the small ones bigger and see what happens up here. 16 is $3.00, 32 is $6.00, 64 is $12.00, and 128 is $24.00. B: It's supposed to be 20 dollars. A: I think it means that the small packets are more expensive.
Do the other method(s); they switch roles for each method.	B: Now we do the divide method. A: OK, what goes over what? B: We can do both. 1.50 by 8 is .18 and 20 divided by 128 is .15. I don't know what that means. A: I think it's how much it costs each ounce. Now the other way. B: 8 by 1.50 is 5.3 and 128 by 20 is 6.4. That's different. A: I think the first one is right cuz in the soda problem, it was money over liters. Money was on top.
Compare their answers; compare the methods, and fix any problems (e.g., if answers are different).	B: That goes with the number lines. So the small packs are .18 each ounce and the big one is .15 each ounce. A: What about the other numbers? B: I don't know. They're ounces over money, so small packs are 5.3 ounces each dollar, maybe? A: And big is 6.4 ounces a dollar. That works! You get more ounces for a dollar.
Compare their answers to their estimates.	B: So that's like three methods. A: Yeah, and they are like our estimates.
Practice sharing a final idea framed by, *With problems like these, you can solve them in two ways. One way is . . . and the other is . . . We noticed that the two methods relate because . . . This problem shows the importance of . . . in math.*	B: So, what will we say? A: With problems like these, you can solve in three ways. You can keep making them bigger on the two number lines. Or you can divide either way. B: But you gotta make sure you know what's over what if you divide. A: I think unit price is the money for each ounce, the small ones. B: Yeah. So divide money by ounces for the unit prices and see which one is less expensive.

Table 4.2 (continued) Math Paired Conversation Protocol with a sample conversation

What and Why Information Gap Math Cards

In this activity, partner A gets a card with the problem on it, without the numbers needed to solve it. Partner B has the data card, which has the information needed to solve the problem. Data cards can also contain shapes, tables, graphs, diagrams, numbers, or key information. (The data card can also contain unnecessary information.) Partner A must think about what is needed to solve the problem and then ask for the information that B has and explain why it's needed. Obviously, there is an information gap that students need to bridge by orally exchanging information, and their reasoning. You can easily create the cards by taking the numbers out of any word problem that you already use.

1. *Read.* The partner with the problem card (partner A) reads his or her card silently and thinks about what information is needed. Partner B reads the data card silently. They should sit side by side, but they shouldn't show or read their cards to each other.

2. *Clarify.* Partner A summarizes or paraphrases the problem (without reading it aloud) to partner B. Partner B asks clarifying questions and paraphrases the situation back to A so that both are clear on what is happening.

3. *Question.* A then asks B for one piece of specific information (e.g., a quantity such as the speed at which the shuttle is moving) that is needed to solve the problem.

4. *Prompt.* When partner A asks for something, partner B should ask for justification— "Why do you need that information?"—before telling the information to partner A. B should ask for justification, even if B already assumes he or she knows it.

5. *Justify.* Partner A justifies the request, and B decides whether the justification is solid and clear enough to give the data to A. You can encourage student A to start with more complex sentences such as "In order to . . . , I need . . . " Because I need to . . . , I need to know . . ." or "Without that information, I can't . . ." (If A gets stuck or doesn't ask for the information on card B, student B can say, "I don't have that, but I do have _____. How might that help you?")

6. *Solve.* Partner A tries to solve the problem and explains his or her procedures. Partner B keeps asking *Why?* along the way. Partner B can also help when partner A gets stuck.

7. *Build.* Finally, both students decide how this problem and its solution methods are examples of one or more mathematical concepts or principles. And, if there is time, they can then work together to write their own problem that requires the solver to use similar methods. This reverse engineering of a problem further builds up their conceptual understandings.

Here is an example of A and B cards in an eighth-grade algebra class, followed by a conversation based on their use (see Figure 4.2).

A: Model

A shuttle enters an orbital path to catch up to an important satellite that isn't working properly. The shuttle is going faster than the satellite and mission control wants to know when the shuttle will reach it.

B: Model

- Shuttle is orbiting at 16,800 mph
- Satellite orbits at 16,000 mph
- Shuttle enters orbit 1,200 miles behind the satellite
- Orbit is 400 miles from the Earth's surface

Figure 4.2 Sample A and B cards in an eighth-grade algebra class

(1)   A: Do you know how fast the shuttle is orbiting?

(2)   B: Yes, but why do you want to know that?

(3)   A: Cuz I need to know it to figure out how long it takes to catch the satellite.

(4)   B: How will knowing the speed help you do that?

(5)   A: I'll use it and the satellite speed and the distance.

(6)   B: What will you do, exactly?

(7)   A: OK, look. The satellite is ahead, but going slower. The shuttle is catching up. So I multiply the speed I get from you by the time for one equation. Then I get the other speed, of the satellite. And I make another equation. OK?

(8)   B: OK, the shuttle is going 16,800 miles per hour.

(9)   A: Thanks. And how fast is the satellite going?

(10) B: Why do you need to know that?

(11) A: To know how long it'll take. I'll make the second equation and put them equal to each other cuz that's where they meet.

(12) B: That makes sense. The satellite's going 16,000 miles per hour.

(13) A: Thanks. And how far are they apart when the shuttle starts its orbit?

(14) B: Why?

Math Type 2: Collaborating to create new math problems

Most traditional models of math instruction do not encourage students to come up with their own problems. However, I encourage you to try it out and see its benefits, even if it gets a little zany at times. Many students want to add their creativity and interests to their learning, which means they put more energy (and learning) into the process when they get a chance to do so. When students work together to create a problem, they need to negotiate both language and math at the same time. That is, as well as handling the numbers, they also both work on language to clarify what is happening in the problem, making it clear enough for others in the class to understand and solve.

To create problems (that help them learn math), students apply the math they have learned to real-world settings and, in a sense, reverse engineer the problems. In doing so, they build a better understanding of the math and how different kinds of problems work. For example, I might tell pairs to create a problem that requires extrapolating data using a linear equation (e.g., predicting future earnings). Both of them contribute ideas and then decide which would make for the most interesting problem for their classmates to solve. I tell them to make sure they set up what is happening and use consistent units. First they need to think of and describe a situation that uses linear equations. Then they need to think about what would happen in the problem to require multiplying rather than addition, subtraction, division, and so on. By the end of their purposeful conversation, the students will have used a hefty amount of mathematical thinking and language.

Here is a conversation from fourth grade. The prompt was, *We have been looking at problems that give you the area and one side of a rectangle, and the reader needs to solve for the missing side. With your partner, come up with an interesting problem that does this.*

(1)	A:	Like that problem with the pool. We can do something like that.
(2)	B:	Maybe something about the turtles like in science, where they lay eggs.
(3)	A:	How?
(4)	B:	They close off areas. Maybe we make it a rectangle.
(5)	A:	Yeah. And so we gotta make up an area.
(6)	B:	Huh?
(7)	A:	He said start with an area. We make it up.
(8)	B:	How about 40.
(9)	A:	40 what?
(10)	B:	Yeah. 40 meters squared.
(11)	A:	OK, but what do we, they gotta find. Like, what's the question?
(12)	B:	Maybe they gotta put a rope around it, you know, to keep people from walking on the eggs. So we gotta know the long and short sides . . . it's a rectangle.
(13)	A:	Yeah. So the long is 10 and the short is 4.
(14)	B:	Yeah, but we can't give both of 'em. We gotta make a person do math to get an answer *[laughs]*.
(15)	A:	OK, so we just give the 10. That makes them find the 4.
(16)	B:	Or we could do 8 and 5. That makes 40.
(17)	A:	Yeah, maybe that's harder.
(18)	B:	So now let's write it.

This type of conversation also helps students learn as teachers, in a sense. They collaborate and use their mathematical background knowledge (in this case, the area of a rectangle) to design a problem. But they are also developing their language skills: when they design the problem, they need to use language as a tool for creation, not just evaluation. As they converse, they refine their language at the word, sentence, and paragraph levels.

Math Type 3: Collaborating to explore, experiment with, and express mathematical concepts

This type of conversation is even rarer than the others. It is focused on deepening and clarifying key mathematical concepts and big ideas. While it may seem to be counterintuitive to allow students to play with mathematical ideas, these conversations can be groundbreaking and foundational for many. Such conversations allow students to take more ownership of math, rather than always feeling that they are behind, catching up, or jumping through the teacher's hoops. For example, a fifth-grade teacher gave students this prompt: *In pairs, collaborate to come up with a presentation for other students on the topic of how to add fractions with unlike denominators. Ask "why" questions a lot. Use different problems as examples.* Students played with different problems, models, and representations to show others the idea. Here is a sample conversation.

(1)	A:	We gotta add fractions.
(2)	B:	**Not the easy ones. The hard ones that are different on the bottom.**
(3)	A:	So when they are different, you gotta change the second one, here, to have the same on the bottom.
(4)	B:	**The same denominator.**
(5)	A:	Whatever you call it. But you can't change it too much.
(6)	B:	**What do you mean?**
(7)	A:	It's the same fraction, but it has different numbers.
(8)	B:	**Huh?**
(9)	A:	Here. Look. We wanna add ¼ and ½ right? So ¼ of a pizza plus a ½ pizza. We gotta change/
(10)	B:	**/Yeah. Change the 2 to a 4 so they're the same. So change it to ¼.**

> (11) A: OK/
>
> (12) B: /But wait. It can't change so much. It needs to be a half, not a quarter.
>
> (13) A: I think we do the same thing to the top and bottom. So it looks different, but it's not different.
>
> (14) B: And that's what we teach?
>
> (15) A: Yeah.

Notice how these students dug into the conceptual reasoning needed to understand the math as they prepared to explain it to others. They made up their own problem as a model and used plenty of language along the way. In line 13, they even used a key mathematical principle: not changing the value of the fraction. Also, the conversation likely helped prepare them for sharing the poster they were creating.

Consider how your students might work together to experiment and play with key math concepts and tools in order to better understand them, without all the pressure of getting the right answer to a problem.

Other purposeful math tasks include the following:

- Design a poster that explains how to find the volume of objects.
- Show how to derive the quadratic equation.
- Show two different ways to solve time-distance problems.
- Act out, with props, how and why to balance both sides of an equation when solving for a variable.
- Design an interesting school (or park, etc.) that stays under budget and yet meets the needs of its users.
- Come up with a business idea and project the minimum you need to make after a year to break even. You must take out a loan at a current interest rate.
- Come up with a fun math lesson to teach what we are currently learning about. I will use it next year.
- Find an environmental issue that uses statistics (space junk, global warming, ocean garbage, endangered species, etc.) and offer possible solutions using statistics.

We need to keep pushing for this shift toward more and better mathematical reasoning in lessons, despite the many ingrained ideas about learning in math that focus on getting the right answers as quickly and easily as possible.

With respect to language development in math, it is very difficult to identify the exact words and sentences that you want students to produce. Granted, there are many math-specific terms that you want students to use, but when you start thinking about what language you want them to use to describe their reasoning, it gets much harder to list. The goal, therefore, should be to create engaging tasks that challenge students to use lots of reasoning and its language with one another, even though you cannot frame up or keep track of all the language used. When we overdo the language piece at the expense of understanding what the language describes, we end up putting the cart before the horse.

Conversations in Science

Science lessons can be a paradise for rich conversations. A wide range of thinking skills and language are needed to do science collaboratively and to build up the many ideas that result from scientific inquiry. It helps to have an overall sense of what scientists tend to talk about. For example, scientists often talk about the following:

- How to solve scientific problems (e.g., *How can we minimize evaporation from open reservoirs?*)
- How to design an effective experiment that proves a hypothesis or answers a tough question
- How to interpret data
- How to write up a lab report or article that clearly describes the process used, the data found, and the importance of the findings (e.g., *an article that describes a lab that showed how water expands when warmed*)
- How to explain or teach a process or concept to others (e.g., *Each pair shares their focal project with others who provide questions and feedback*)
- How to apply what they are learning to real life

Within the four main domains of science taught in school (physical, life, Earth and space, and engineering design), there are many opportunities for engaging in academic conversations. The Next Generation Science Standards emphasize using key, skills including communication, collaboration, inquiry, problem solving, and flexibility. Effective conversations are full of these things.

Even though students can have many types of conversations about science, including argumentation-based ones such as those in Chapter 3, I focus on three types in this section: (1) collaborating to design experiments and interpret the data, (2) collaborating to explain scientific phenomena, and (3) science role-based improvisation conversations. I provide a description of each type with sample conversations.

Science Type 1: Collaborating to design experiments and interpret data

Conversations can help students think like scientists. Most scientists do some observing or wondering about a topic or phenomenon and then create a hypothesis about causes and effects. Then they design experiments to check what they found against their hypotheses or to learn something that they didn't expect. In most experiments, scientists identify variables and keep all of them constant except the one that they think is the cause.

There is a lot to talk about when setting up an experiment. For example, in observing that a light bulb changes intensity as different materials are used to complete the circuit, two students might hypothesize that different metals do not conduct electricity in the same way. The students then converse about the variables that need to remain constant, such as batteries, wires, connections, temperature, and the bulb, in order to make a solid conclusion. As they think about metals that might have similar but not the same conductivity, they decide that they want a more precise way to measure voltage than just looking at the bulb. They ask the teacher for a voltmeter. They then design a series of trials with different materials. During and after the experiment, students must interpret the results and explain what happened between variables.

Even if the experiment is not possible at the school (e.g., living in outer space, life around an oceanic thermal vent), just having students think about and design experiments is worth the time. For example, you might have students design an experiment that scientists could do to understand the influence of carbon emissions on the atmosphere.

Labs are also common in many science classes. They are typically already organized, with steps and procedures to follow. They are less flexible and develop fewer inquiry and experiment skills, but they can be focused and educational. They can produce a variety of topics for academic conversations and ideas for experiments. For example, after or during a squid dissection lab, students can converse about why the squid developed certain adaptations over time. In a lab on acids and bases, students can converse about the applications of the reactions they observed, as well as the chemical causes and effects.

As student scientists infer and conclude, they must also be able to accurately describe their levels of certainty. Students must be able to differentiate strong from weak data patterns and be able to objectively describe the strength of the conclusions that they make from such data. And as students mature, they need to get better at analyzing and critiquing the quality of experimental procedures, data gathering, different ways of interpreting data, and presenting conclusions. All of these skills can improve as a result of having rich conversations.

Here is a sample conversation from eighth grade. The prompt was, *Design a scale model experiment that helps you see if the light car or the heavy truck has more energy when at the top of a hill. I want you to use the terms* potential energy *and* kinetic energy, *if you can.*

(1)	A:	OK. They are not moving at the top.
(2)	B:	They got potential energy up there.
(3)	A:	The truck is heavier, so it's got more, right?
(4)	B:	Yeah, but we gotta show it. An experiment. They gotta do something.
(5)	A:	So we let them go down the hill.
(6)	B:	What will that do?
(7)	A:	I don't know. But what else can they do?
(8)	B:	Wait. Yeah. OK. They go down the hill, like a race, and we see the one that wins.
(9)	A:	How will it help?
(10)	B:	The one that wins has more energy.
(11)	A:	How do we know?
(12)	B:	It takes energy to move, like gas. It didn't have gas, but had potential energy. And it turned into moving energy.
(13)	A:	Kinetic?
(14)	B:	Yeah. OK. So that's it.
(15)	A:	OK.

Notice the robust mental processing of the science concepts, the ownership and development of an idea, and how they talked as scientists would co-design the simple experiment. In this case, I would have liked some longer turns and more explanation, but that is something to work on the next time they have this type of conversation.

Science Type 2: Collaborating to explain scientific phenomena

We can't design or do experiments every day in science class. We also need to do a fair amount of modeling, labs, videos, presentations, projects, and learning from texts. Students need to be able to learn complex scientific ideas from such lessons and, as it happens, conversations can help. Remember that conversations provide an opportunity for students to try out their evolving ideas on others and to hear (a) how others respond to these ideas (*Awesome! Huh?*) and (b) how the others are thinking about the topic.

Most of the time, the final product of the conversation is to come up with a superclear and engaging way to describe or explain the concept. Students can use any number of strategies found in this and other chapters. The students in the following conversation used the Building Ideas Visual described in Chapter 2. This conversation is from sixth grade and the prompt was, *Come up with a clear way to teach others about how shifts in tectonic plates cause earthquakes. Use your Building Ideas Visual notes to help you and your partner continue to build up your ideas.*

(1)	A:	What bricks do you have?
(2)	B:	I got that they stick together.
(3)	A:	What?
(4)	B:	The plates. They move next to each other and they stick, like this *[makes fists and puts knuckles together, moving hands in a shear motion]*. Then finally they unstick. Boom! And you got an earthquake.
(5)	A:	Why?
(6)	B:	They come apart superfast and it shakes. But I don't know how we can teach it.
(7)	A:	Maybe we get two pieces of wood. And the sides are like jagged, like a saw, so they stick and we move them. Then we/
(8)	B:	/And we could get big pieces of wood and have a person stand on it. So then we move them. They unlock, and it shakes them.
(9)	A:	I like it. But I also have a brick with a drawing. It has a plate sliding under another plate, like this (*bumps one flat hand into the other and slides one hand underneath*).
(10)	B:	Maybe we can do that with the boards, too.
(11)	A:	Yeah, we push 'em at each other.

Again, notice the ownership and engagement as students are encouraged to work together to *do* science, rather than just memorize it. And, in this case, the process of coming up with a way to teach a concept to others helps solidify it even more in the minds of the students.

Science Type 3: Science role-based conversations

This type of conversation allows students to be a little more creative and dramatic, while supporting the learning of science and its language. Students take on the role of two related or contrasting objects, people, or processes in science and have a conversation in those roles. For example, a river might talk to a glacier, a reptile might chat with a mammal, an earthquake with a volcano, Mercury with Jupiter, a lake with an ocean, the sun with the moon, a crocodile with a shark, a dinosaur with a bird, or a sound wave with a light wave. Here is the procedure with some tips:

1. Pick two topics, processes, or objects that, if they could talk to one another, would generate an interesting conversation. You can also have students brainstorm and choose two roles that would be productive.
2. Ask students what they think the two things might discuss. Come up with a prompt that will inspire as much conversation as possible. (*You are a river and a glacier and you are deciding which of you has done more to shape the geography of the Earth. You are a light wave talking to a sound wave. Find out what you have in common and how you are different.*)
3. Optionally, you can have students use visual organizers that remind them of the concepts they should talk about in their roles. Sentence frames can also help support the language: "I think we are different in several ways. For example, you . . . and I . . . We seem to have some things in common, like . . ."

Here is a sample fourth-grade conversation between a river and a glacier. The teacher had them start with *Tell me about yourself. What do you do?* and then move to *How are we different and similar?* and finally to *Now let's decide which one of us has done more for the geography of Earth.* Make sure to spend time on one topic first. Then move on to the other and compare.

(1)	A:	Tell me about yourself. What do you do?
(2)	B:	I'm a river. I go down valleys.
(3)	A:	How do you change the land?
(4)	B:	I keep on washing down rocks and dirt, like digging it down.
(5)	A:	Is there a good example of that?
(6)	B:	Yeah. The Grand Canyon. I don't know where it is, but the river made it. What about you?
(7)	A:	I'm a glacier. I'm a big bunch of ice. I think it's a lot of snow.
(8)	B:	What do you do?
(9)	A:	I move, but slow. And I make, I don't know, valleys, too. But also bays for water.
(10)	B:	How?
(11)	A:	I'm heavy, so I push rocks and dirt in front. Then when I melt, it fills with water.
(12)	B:	So how are we different and similar?
(13)	A:	We move.
(14)	B:	And we have water in us.
(15)	A:	But you have water and I have ice. That's different.
(16)	B:	And we dig up land.
(17)	A:	But I think you do more, like to change land. You did the Grand Canyon, and there are rivers everywhere.
(18)	B:	I agree.

You can see the engaging nature of playing roles and the many turns that were facilitated by the structure. Also, their content was pretty accurate. Notice, too, the language of questioning, describing, personifying (using the pronoun *I*), and clarifying.

Conversations in History and Social Studies

Social studies and history classes can be opportunities for students to discuss a range of meaningful topics. Teachers can provide prompts that encourage students to bring their values, perspectives, experiences, and backgrounds into the classroom as they build up important ideas.

With respect to history, students can work on the following historical thinking skills in their conversations: understanding multiple perspectives and motives, using primary and secondary sources and inferring biases in them, and comparing and contrasting interpretations using multiple primary sources.

With respect to social studies (social studies, government, economics, etc.), students need to understand culture and its influences on social processes and institutions, political processes and structures, and economic processes and forces. Conversations can help students dig into these understandings, and they can also help students see that they can contribute to making the world a better place, especially if they understand how the world works.

In addition to having students converse about argumentation-based issues (see Chapter 3), you can work on three engaging types of conversations in history and social studies: (1) collaborating to explain events, systems, and people; (2) collaborating to apply lessons from history to the present; and (3) collaborating to solve a social or political problem (including through project-based learning).

History/Social Studies Type 1: Collaborating to explain events, systems, and people

Historians tend to interpret events in the past and then argue their causes, effects, and importance. Social scientists tend to study how groups of people live, which includes governments, traditions, beliefs, and social systems. And while the big events and famous people often get the bulk of the attention in both subjects, it is also important to understand the wide range of perspectives of people from different socioeconomic classes, genders, racial groups, ethnicities, and linguistic backgrounds. Students need to learn how history and social issues can be seen from different points of view, and how more inclusive stories of less famous people are also highly valuable. Students can collaborate in conversations to better explore these events, concepts, and perspectives.

Prompts should push students to explain causes and effects, relationships, and motivations. Here are a few examples:

- Whose perspective is this account of the event showing? Whose story is *not* being told?
- Should we learn about ordinary people in the past? How can we learn more about ordinary people?
- What helped George Washington to be chosen as the first president?

- What motivates people to move permanently to other places—even places where the language and culture are very different?
- How can we make our country a better place with respect to reducing the injustice, inequality, and racism that still exist?
- How did Martin Luther King Jr. influence the history of the United States?
- Why did Christopher Columbus sail across the Atlantic Ocean?
- Should we vote on every decision in our class? In our country?
- Why do we have local, state, and national governments? Do they work?

Here is a conversation from tenth-grade world history class. The prompt was, *Build up an idea that connects the concepts of tyranny and rule of law . . . and why they were so important in the late 1700s.*

(1)	A:	So, what was tyranny?
(2)	B:	It's like a bad king who taxes you and tries to control everything.
(3)	A:	What's an example?
(4)	B:	The guy in North Korea, I think.
(5)	A:	So, what about rule of law?
(6)	B:	I think it means everyone has to follow the law?
(7)	A:	I have here, Aristotle said, "It is more proper that law should govern than any one of the citizens."
(8)	B:	So I think people were tired of kings and tyrants who didn't follow laws. They wanted it to be fair.
(9)	A:	So the rule of law was a way to fight against tyranny.
(10)	B:	Not like with guns, but ideas. For a long time it was all about kings. Like we learned last week about the "divine rights" that kings said they had, and all they did to keep on being kings.
(11)	A:	And Locke said we all have rights to life, liberty, and property.
(12)	B:	So its importance?
(13)	A:	I think it got revolutions going, like in France and the US.
(14)	B:	How? And why then? Why not earlier?
(15)	A:	I don't know. Maybe . . . Let's ask.

In this conversation there are the beginnings of a more robust understanding of how the concepts were related and their importance. I would have liked a few more examples, and a more extensive explanation of the importance of the topic, but this is still a decent start to understanding how the development of ideas played key roles in history. And the conversation also seemed to get them more interested in asking key questions related to why things happened at certain times and not others (line 14). This fosters ownership and interest in history. Next, I would pair them with several other partners on this same topic and see what happens. (For more information on engaging history lessons, check out resources at the California History-Social Science Project, chssp.ucdavis.edu, and the Stanford History Education Group, sheg.stanford.edu.)

History/Social Studies Type 2: Collaborating to apply lessons from history

We have a responsibility to teach students how to learn from history to improve the present and future. They need to learn about the successes and failures of the past to keep doing the things that lead to successes and avoid doing the things that lead to failures. We want them to be better at this than we have been. We also want them to apply lessons to other time periods as well as other locations. We want them to recognize possible patterns that might help them to understand causes, effects, and meaning across time and space.

For many students who are not naturally interested in the stories of the past for their own sake, applying history lessons can increase their engagement and develop a key skill at the same time. Here are some examples of lessons from history that are worthy of application—and conversation:

- If there are resources, some people will want more than their fair share.
- Rich and powerful people strive to stay rich and powerful.
- History is written by the "winners."
- Historical sources, primary and secondary, are often full of bias and lies.
- Democracy is much more fragile than we think it is.
- History repeats itself—especially when people (a) don't remember the lessons of the past, (b) don't intervene, or (c) benefit from it.
- Change can happen nonviolently.
- All civilizations rise and fall.
- Ordinary citizens can make a big difference, especially if they work together.
- All people are equal and should be free.

For example, fifth-grade history students had been using a graphic organizer like the one in Table 4.3. The class had initially worked together with the teacher to fill in some of the boxes in their visuals. The historical lesson (principle, theme) to be applied was on the top, supported by past examples and present applications below.

HISTORICAL LESSON TO APPLY: All people are equal and should be free.	
PAST	**PRESENT**
Declaration of Independence (all men are created equal)	Poor, not free; health insurance
Lincoln's quotes and Civil War	Modern-day slavery and human trafficking
Women couldn't vote	Women get lower pay in same jobs

Table 4.3 Graphic organizer: historical lesson chart

Here is a sample conversation. The prompt was, *OK, use your historical lesson chart to have a conversation that builds up a solid application of the past to the present. What does the lesson mean for us now?*

(1) A: What do you think?

(2) B: About what?

(3) A: About the lesson from history.

(4) B: All people are equal? Yeah. I agree.

(5) A: Yeah, me too. But we gotta talk about why. Like the Declaration of Independence says all men are created equal and have life, liberty, and happiness.

(6) B: It didn't say women.

(7) A: No, but it should have.

(8) B: And it should have been for African American men, but it wasn't. I guess cuz they were slaves?

(9)   A: I think people were more racist back then. Slavery was legal. Jefferson had slaves. And he wrote the Declaration!

(10) B: Why were they so racist?

(11) A: Things were different. They/

(12) B: /So? That doesn't make it right. Slavery is never OK.

(13) A: I think slave owners were selfish. I think they knew it was wrong but wanted to make more money.

(14) B: And it's still happening. Human trafficking. They find people who want to work and turn them into slaves. Millions of people. Even here. And a lot are women and children. It's so wrong.

(15) A: How can people be like that? People who do that to others.

(16) B: It's evil and/.

(17) A: /I don't get it. Freedom is so important, like it said in the Declaration, but it is, there are thousands, like the article said 50,000 are in it.

(18) B: We should help.

The use of the organizer got them going and helped them stay focused on the lesson to apply. Also notice the productive emotions that emerged from building up this lesson. They did a nice job elaborating on the topic of slavery, supporting and clarifying the idea that all people are created equal, and applying it to modern-day human trafficking. Student B did interrupt a couple of times, and I might remind him afterward to wait until a partner's turn ends. After this conversation, I would have students find a different partner and engage in conversation about other examples on the graphic organizer that they didn't talk about in the first conversation (e.g., women, the poor, Lincoln).

History/Social Studies Type 3: Collaborating to solve social problems and challenges

In trying to solve a real issue or challenge, students tend to become much more motivated to learn and remember more about the topic. There is usually a lot of critical thinking as solution ideas are posed and weighed for their potential in solving the problem. It is exciting to see students taking on real issues that affect them and their future—and all the learning that results from the process.

A larger-scale version of this type of conversation is project-based learning. Students typically do research on a significant question or problem in order to address it. There should be many conversations along the way that help students refine and build up the ideas that go into their final product.

In a nutshell, students engage in creative and collaborative problem solving in this kind of conversation, just as adults do in many professions. Students pose or choose problems and then jointly discuss ideas based on the following steps. Encourage them to choose (or give them) a topic that requires a creative way to solve a problem or express a complex idea to others. Give options, if possible (e.g., increasing how we show respect and responsibility at our school, dealing with bullies at school, reducing cheating in school, reducing the use of bad language, reducing the use of violent video games by students in school, solving a local pollution problem, helping homeless people, saving the rain forests). Model the process before they start it for themselves.

1. Clarify the problem. Students make sure they can define the problem to others, describe why it is a problem, and explain what will change if the problem is solved.

2. Brainstorm possible solution ideas without critique. Any idea, within reason, is accepted and written down. This can be done as a whole class at first, and then eventually students will do this independently of you.

3. Narrow the solution ideas down with critical thinking and criteria. Have students decide whether it is possible to use any of the solutions. They can talk about the high cost of certain solutions, long-term versus short-term value, and so on.

4. Zoom in on two solution ideas and compare their merits, limits, rationales, evidence, potentials, and any past similar examples that worked or not. (See Chapter 3 for more on how to evaluate and choose.)

5. Work together to choose the best solution and discuss how to implement it.

6. Have students collaborate to write or present their solution idea for a realistic audience.

Here is a conversation excerpt from a ninth-grade social studies class that was studying world religions. Several students mentioned reading news stories of discrimination against people because of their religious beliefs. These two students chose to tackle the problem of religious intolerance and discrimination.

(1) A: So, what's the problem?

(2) B: People treat different religions badly. Discrimination on religion. Like the government doesn't let them come into our country. Or they don't give them jobs or they yell things at them.

(3) A: OK, so what are ways to fix that?

(4) B: We can join protests.

(5) A: Yeah. Or we could send letters to government people.

(6) B: But how can we like get people, even people here at school, to see it's wrong? I've heard people make jokes about other students.

(7) A: They gotta get to know people from other religions.

(8) B: Why?

(9) A: Because they will see how nice they are. I have a Jewish friend and my stepsister has a Muslim friend. They are great. And I feel bad for them.

(10) B: Me too. What if we have a party that celebrates different religions/

(11) A: /and countries where they are from. And they bring special foods and maybe share something special to teach everyone about their culture. And we can/

(12) B: /But what about money, like the cost?

(13) A: Maybe we have it here at school. And people bring their own food to share.

(14) B: And we have a time to mix and get to know each other. Maybe play some games.

(15) A: I like it. So, why do we think this idea is best?

(16) B: Maybe it doesn't change the government from closing off the country to others, but I think it's the only way to beat discrimination like this, against religions. And maybe someone at our party becomes president someday.

Notice how these students came up with a solid solution and justified choosing it at the end. Notice the large amount of language used and the many phrases and terms that they will use the rest of their lives. And notice how this conversation, while it might not directly raise their standardized test scores, might be one of the many enduring interactions that is used by each student to build themselves up into the amazing people they were born to be.

Conclusion

This long chapter was just a brief taste of the great conversations that are happening in our schools. Conversations in every content area are not just helpful, they are vital. They are vital for improving content learning, conversation skills, and language use.

Chapter 5

Assessing Conversations

*When you know where you are,
a map becomes much more useful.*

If you have ever tried to assess a conversation, even just one among the many going on at once in your classroom, you know how challenging it is. And at the same time you also know how useful it can be to observe students talking about the content they are learning.

Most of this chapter describes formative assessment practices, which tend to be ongoing and less formal. This type of assessment includes short observations over the shoulders of two students who are talking, the observation of oral language activities that use conversation skills, and even student writing that results from conversations.

Look at the following sixth-grade conversation and see what kinds of information about students you can gain from it. The prompt was, *Why was having surplus crops so important for the rise of civilizations?*

(1)   A: They had extra food to trade it for things.

(2)   B: How is that good for cities and civilizations?

(3)   A: It's like, remember, other people who don't want to farm can make other things, like carts and hammers.

(4)   B: Oh yeah, they can get good at making those things, or doing skills like building houses, like people do today. Like we get all our food at the store.

(5)	A:	OK, so the farmers sell what they don't eat for things and money.
(6)	B:	For example?
(7)	A:	For example, a farmer grows lots of grapes, keeps some, and sells the rest.
(8)	B:	So then?
(9)	A:	I guess you got more jobs and buildings around and then you want people to, like to have police and roads, and you need a government for that.
(10)	B:	So taxes.
(11)	A:	What do you mean?
(12)	B:	So extra money that they have they pay taxes for the government. And government gets bigger, and so you have a civilization.
(13)	A:	OK.

Even without having been in this classroom or knowing the students, what did you learn? You saw a lot of content knowledge, academic thinking, and the building of an idea with clarifying and supporting. They could have clarified and supported a bit more in some turns, and I might have wanted more specific examples from the units (Mesopotamia, Egypt, etc.) that they had been studying. But overall, it is effective enough to be worth the time, and I got some good insights for next steps.

These two students could talk about the same prompt tomorrow and the conversation might be different. And the conversations will vary even more widely if you change the topic, content area, or partners. There are some skills that we should look for in all conversations. Yet there are many other skills and knowledge that will vary, depending on your students and what they are learning. For this reason, I don't include a fixed all-in-one rubric in this chapter. I instead provide a range of features and *look-for's,* so that you can build your own customized observation and analysis tools.

Build Your Own Conversation Assessment Tools

While you might want one big, all-inclusive assessment tool, it would have too many elements to look for and evaluate in a single conversation. A more practical alternative is building tools for various purposes and focuses, such as for looking at the use of nonverbal cues, conversation skills, thinking skills, language, content understandings, or a combination of these. And you can also use different tools for different situations and purposes, such as for your own observations, student self-assessment, instructional rounds, observations by coaches, and summative assessment.

Also, if you have a tool in your hand, there is usually too much to read through and consider as you observe students in real time in a classroom context. I recommend that you use whatever you create on paper for a while to get its basics in your head, and then stop using it while you actually listen.

Dimensions and Features to Assess in Conversations

In this section, I provide a list of dimensions and features to look for and notice in conversations. I do not usually assign points to these, but when I do, I use 0, 1, and 2, for *Not much*, *Some*, and *Plenty* (or similar terms). You can put these into rubrics and use more academic terms to differentiate them, as many rubrics do. Perhaps the most efficient way, though, is not to use evaluative terms or numbers and instead simply have short lists of features in the tool, some of which might stay the same during the year (e.g., clarifying and supporting) and some of which might vary, depending on student needs, the content area, or thinking skills being learned in the unit of study.

Conversation Skills

Because conversation skills are foundational for making conversations work, I put them first. Look for whether and how well students work with other students to build and choose ideas that you want.

How well do students . . .

- create, choose, and pose relevant and useful (buildable) ideas to talk about? How well do they stick to the prompt?
- build ideas? Do students listen to partner turns with a building ideas mindset? Do students know when certain types of "bricks" are needed (e.g., clarifying or supporting) in order to build up each idea as clearly and strongly as possible?
- connect to the previous turns of partners to build up ideas? Do they connect or refer to relevant known and given information and then add appropriate new information that builds up the idea?
- stay relevant and focused in all stages of the conversation? Do they avoid saying ideas that they think are false, silly, irrelevant, or filler?

- clarify thoughts and terms, and know when to prompt for clarification? Do they effectively ask questions, elaborate on key points, define key terms, paraphrase, and/or explain?
- support ideas with evidence and reasoning and know when to prompt for support?
- evaluate the strengths of evidences for an idea in order to decide which evidences are worth keeping and which are too weak to include?
- in an argument, evaluate the evidential strength of the competing ideas?

  How well do they
  - name and use criteria?
  - compare the strengths (weights) and logically choose the strongest (heaviest) idea?
  - explain and negotiate final decisions and conclusions?

- work *with* partners, not against, even if they disagree at times?
- remain open to learning new ideas and having ideas change during conversation?
- interpret and use nonverbal skills when speaking, listening, emphasizing, and questioning?
- value and respect one another's thinking, ideas, values, and priorities? How well do they listen to partner ideas, attitudes, and feelings?

Quantity

While "more is better" doesn't always apply to classroom conversations, many students need to say more in their interactions with others, taking more and longer turns. Often, the more someone says in a conversation, the more information there is to work with. Here are a few things to look for:

- **Are there enough turns in the conversation** to construct one or more ideas?
- **Is each turn long enough?** Should they be longer, with more and longer sentences, in order to be clearer in each turn and clearer for the conversation overall? Do turns contribute an appropriate amount of information that is required at the current stage of the conversation, not way more or way less? (Many students have become accustomed to saying as little as possible, which stifles good conversation. Yet some students tend to say too much in turns.)

- **Do both students talk more or less an equal amount?** Does one student dominate?

Meta-conversation Moves

There is very little research on what I call *meta-conversation moves*, but I think they are worth a mention here. I have noticed in some conversations that students use turns to guide or shape the conversation. These expressions often help to redirect, deepen, or extend conversations. These are expressions such as the following:

- Let's build up the opposite side of the argument.
- We need to use criteria.
- I don't think the prompt is asking that.
- That is an idea we can build up.
- Have we built up the idea enough?
- I think we need more evidence.
- We need to choose an idea to build up.
- I don't think we're done. We need to . . .

I recommend that you encourage and look for these types of moves. You can highlight them and push for their use, but don't force them on students (e.g., don't give points for using them). Just explain that knowing how to have a conversation, and saying these kinds of moves during conversations to build ideas, tends to improve them.

Language

As you have noticed by now in this book, I do not promote extra focusing on correct language for the purpose of sounding fluent or academic. Language should be used to communicate—even if the result rebels against what is often called "standard English" by borrowing from other languages, using colloquial expressions, using incorrect grammar, etc. For example, incomplete sentences can communicate ideas better than complete ones in many cases.

Conversations provide exceptionally rich opportunities to observe how students use language to interact and talk about academic ideas. In every turn you can see how well students are listening and putting their ideas into words. Here are some important language features to look for that can help students communicate better in conversations and beyond. You might add some of your own features based on the standards and what you observe in your students.

To make their turns as clear as possible for partners, how well do students . . .

- use the best and most appropriate words?
- combine words into phrases and sentences?
- connect and organize sentences?
- organize ideas?
- use pronunciation and prosody to express ideas?
- use facial expressions, posture, and gestures?

Content Knowledge and Concepts

We can also gather a lot about the content that students are learning, especially where they are along the continuum of understanding complex concepts.

How well do students . . .

- understand the target objectives and concept(s) of the lesson, unit, and discipline?
- use or allow the conversation to increase content understandings?
- help, nudge, and allow partners to think more deeply about the topic?

Thinking Skills

We can also see how well students are using and developing the key thinking skills of the discipline.

How well do students use disciplinary thinking skills, such as . . .

- *Language arts:* Interpreting, supporting an argument, evaluating, applying, and synthesizing?
- *History and social studies:* Interpreting, identifying causes and effects, comparing, contextualizing, empathizing, recognizing bias, supporting claims, evaluating, and applying?
- *Science*: Interpreting, hypothesizing, identifying causes and effects, identifying variables, supporting claims, solving problems, applying, and making conclusions?
- *Math*: Interpreting, justifying ideas with reasoning, solving problems multiple ways, comparing, evaluating, and applying?

- *Arts*: Interpreting, expressing, solving problems, comparing, empathizing, applying, and synthesizing?

Socio-emotional Dimensions

Here are several additional important socio-emotional dimensions of learning and development that conversations can help us see (from Singer and Zwiers 2016).

- *Power dynamics*. Which voices dominate discussions? Which students are silent, or defer to others? Is participation equitable, or are patterns of race, gender, English proficiency, or some other factor(s) influencing which voices are heard?
- *Perspectives*. What are the varied perspectives, points of view, and opinions that students have on the topic(s) of discussion?
- *Learning approaches*. How does the student approach learning in this discipline and learning in general?
- *Engagement*. How engaged in the topic are students? What questions do they ask?

As you can see, conversations can be very rich sources of information about students and classroom dynamics. You can get many important insights for the price of one analyzed conversation—and for at least two students at the same time!

Sample Assessment Tools

The last section described many areas to assess in one conversation. Here are some sample tools from teachers with whom I work, but what you design for your setting should be tailored to your students' needs. As I wrote earlier, I recommend building a basic tool and memorizing it so it doesn't have to be on paper.

It helps to keep any conversation assessment tool as simple as possible, given how many student conversations are going on at one time. I recommend choosing just a few things from the previous lists. To do this, you can use the following criteria:

a. The most-needed skills and content that you have noticed by informally observing their conversations.
b. The most-needed skills and content that you have noticed from conversation-inspired products (writing, posters, etc.) and from products that can be improved through conversation.

c. The most-needed skills and content based on student interviews and self-assessments.

Sample Assessment Tool: Third Grade

Here is a sample assessment tool created by a third-grade teacher after a month of initial observations of student interactions. The teacher who created this made it for use across the content areas of English language arts, math, science, and social studies.

Students:

❑ Stick to the prompt.
❑ Listen well and build on partner ideas.
❑ Don't talk too much or too little.
❑ Clarify ideas.
❑ Support ideas with text examples.
❑ Work with partners, not against them.
❑ Use positive facial expressions, eye contact, and gestures.
❑ Build up each idea as much as possible.

Let's practice using this sample tool with a snippet of a third-grade conversation. Students had read *Charlotte's Web* (White 1952). The teacher asked them to talk in pairs about what the main themes of the story were.

(1)   A: Maybe a theme is friendship?

(2)   B: What about friendship?

(3)   A: It's good to be friends?

(4)   B: Yeah. I agree, but we already know that, right? Maybe we think about what was new or interesting about friendship in the book.

(5)   A: OK. So one thing is I never knew that pigs and spiders can be friends.

(6)   B: I like that. So for people, like us, what does it mean? Maybe it's you can be friends with people you don't think you'll be friends with.

(7)   A: Yeah. Here's a quote for that: "I've got a new friend, all right! But what a gamble friendship is! Charlotte is fierce, brutal, scheming, bloodthirsty—everything I don't like. How can I learn to like her, even though she is pretty and, of course, clever?" . . . But what does *gamble* mean?

(8)   B: I think it's like, I don't know. Maybe like doing something but you want to or you think it might not work.

(9)   A: That makes sense. But why did Wilbur wanna be friends with her?

(10)   B: Maybe he needed a friend cuz he didn't have Fern anymore.

(11)   A: And he really needed her to use her webs.

(12)   B: What do you mean?

(13)   A: She worked really hard to write those words and it helped save him. He needed her to live.

(14)   B: Yeah. That's part of friendship, too. Helping each other, even when it's hard to.

(15)   A: And he helped her after she died. He brought her eggs back to the farm.

(16)   B: But she was dead.

(17)   A: So? He was still being a good friend. . . . Are we done?

(18)   B: I think so.

The teacher could check most of the boxes in the tool, even based on this short, transcribed snippet of conversation. The tool would then show that these third graders are building a solid foundation of conversation skills and dispositions to prepare them for future conversation-based learning. If the teacher wanted to gather even more information, she could put evaluative numbers (1, 2, 3) to each box and add written observation notes next to them. This would help her provide more feedback to students and inform instruction.

Sample Assessment Tool: Seventh-Grade History

Here is a student conversation and a sample assessment tool from a seventh-grade history teacher. This tool has a teacher component so that she can reflect on her teaching and support during and after the lesson. For fun, cover up what the teacher wrote in the "Strengths" and "Needs" columns in Table 5.1 and take your own notes. Then compare notes.

The following conversation was prompted by the question, *Were the results of the crusades more positive or negative?*

(1)   A: I don't know. Let's build up both sides.

(2)   B: OK, the positive first.

(3)   A: So, it changed Europe.

(4)   B: How?

(5)   A: I read that it made transportation better.

(6)   B: How?

(7)   A: They had to make better ships and land things to move the armies over there, East.

(8)   B: That's good. What else?

(9)   A: You say something.

(10) B: OK, so I read that kings got more power and it stopped feudalism.

(11) A: OK, what's feudalism? And why's it good to stop it?

(12) B: It was like little castles all around and they would fight a lot. Like little countries, I think.

(13) A: Why'd the crusades stop it?

(14) B: A lot of knights that had the castles died, so the king got their land.

(15) A: OK. And another good thing is the stuff they brought back: spices and perfume and silk.

(16) B: OK, what about the bad?

(17) A: Lots of people died. On both sides.

(18) B: And lots of Jews died, too.

(19) A: Why?

(20) B: This article says that the Christians went across Europe and killed Jews cuz they weren't Christians.

(21) A: Why? I don't get why religions kill other religions.

(22) B: Yeah. Religion is supposed to make people better and nicer. OK, crusades, bad.

(23) A: They also ruined a lot of places in the Middle East, and took land away from the Muslims in Spain. It wasn't theirs.

(24) B: Yeah. I think all that stealing and killing make the crusades more bad than good.

(25) A: I agree.

STUDENTS . . .	STRENGTHS	NEEDS
Co-build up idea(s) to be as clear and strong as possible	Focused on building both sides	
Clarify ideas (define, paraphrase, synthesize)	Asked good clarify questions (How/Why)	
Support ideas with evidence, especially from primary sources	Good evidence from secondary sources	They need to use primary sources
Understand the target concept(s) of the lesson or unit	Solid evidence for both sides	
Students use history thinking skills: • *Interpret primary sources* • *Identify causes and effects* • *Recognize biases in sources*	Cause/effect OK (transportation, end of feudalism)	Need primary sources
Teacher—Did I . . .		
Create an engaging purpose for conversing? And did I make sure that students had enough to talk about?	Yes (engaging argument focused on content)	
Provide effective modeling and scaffolding of conversation and history skills?		I need to model and push for primary source use
Provide language support to help students communicate their ideas?		Next time I will model how to explain why evidence is positive or negative

Table 5.1 Sample conversation assessment tool

Notice how the use of a tool can inform next steps for teacher and students alike. For example, in the last row, the teacher saw the need to help students do a better job of explaining why or how evidence was positive or negative.

Sample Peer and Self-Assessment Tools

Given that many conversations often happen simultaneously in a lesson, the more we cultivate in students the abilities to assess their conversation skills on their own, the better. Work with your students to construct self-assessment tools that are based on the tools that you are using. You can work as a class to practice their use with sample conversations. For example, one teacher I know video-recorded conversations and had the entire class assess the recorded conversations using the tools they had co-created.

Peer and self-assessment allows students to take ownership of the ideas that they are learning. You and your students can modify the assessments that you are using to create self- and peer-assessment tools that are student-friendly. You might, for example, start with a tool that is focused on certain skills such as clarifying and supporting. Then you or they add tools or rows with other features during the year.

Sample Conversation Self-Assessment

Here is a sample conversation and self-assessment tool (Table 5.2) from a fourth-grade science class. Imagine that you are student A and use the tool to self-assess your conversation, considering both the strengths and weaknesses to work on. Don't worry about the rows that you can't observe here. The prompt was, *The principal is listening to a message on her cell phone. Where did the energy used to create that sound come from?*

(1)   A: From the cell phone charger, right?

(2)   B: But before that?

(3)   A: From the electric wires, like from the power station.

(4)   B: But where does the power station get its energy?

(5)   A: I don't know.

(6)   B: Maybe from dams, like in that picture.

(7)   A: How does water make electricity?

(8)   B: It turns those round things around. I don't know.

(9) A: So the water has energy cuz it's up high. How's it get up there?

(10) B: The rivers. But you mean how does it get into the rivers, right?

(11) A: Yeah. Rain. So but that water comes from maybe lakes and the ocean/

(12) B: /Yeah, and the sun heats it up. It's that water cycle.

(13) A: So the sun starts it.

	WELL	OK	NEED TO IMPROVE
I thought about how buildable the initial idea(s) that I or my partner posed.			*Yes*
I clarified meanings and asked my partner to clarify, when needed or when in doubt.	*Asked clarify questions*		
I supported ideas with examples and evidence and asked my partner for support when needed.		*Yes*	
We stayed focused on building an idea (or on both ideas, one after the other, if an argument).	*Yes, to answer the question*		
I valued my partner's ideas and showed with my body and eyes that I was listening.		*I listened*	

Table 5.2 Sample self-assessment tool

Sample Peer Assessment of Conversations

You can also have students meet in groups of three, where one student is the coach who uses a tool to observe and provide feedback to the other two, who are talking. Then they switch roles. Here is a sample conversation in eighth-grade language arts after students had read *Flowers for Algernon* (Keyes 1966). Cover up the notes on the right-hand side and try taking the role of a peer who uses the sample peer assessment tool (Table 5.3) to write down positive aspects and things to work on in the conversation. Then compare notes.

(1)   A: Why do you think the author wrote this story?

(2)   B: Maybe to teach us we should be who we're born to be.

(3)   A: What do you mean?

(4)   B: You know, in the story Charlie wants to be smart, and his operation makes him smarter. But it's not natural. And he wasn't happy, even after he's smart.

(5)   A: Yeah. And he was kinda like a science experiment. I don't think they should experiment on people. It's maybe like when they experiment on animals.

(6)   B: Yeah. It's messed up. What about the other side?

(7)   A: Maybe it's that we can be smart, all of us. And maybe it's OK when science helps? Science helps people be better in lots of ways.

(8)   B: What's an example?

(9)   A: Like drugs. When we are sick, they help cure us. I took pills last year when I had a infection, and they made me better.

(10) B: I guess. And I think it's good to see, like, people like him could be smart.

(11) A: What do you mean?

(12) B: Like I see people like him, like at school, and I think they're just, I don't know, broken. But inside they're like us, maybe smarter than us.

(13) A: Maybe, OK, so are we done with both sides?

(14) B: Yeah. Now we gotta decide which is heaviest.

(15) A: I can't decide. I don't think it's natural and it was like an experiment on a person/

(16) B: /But it also, like I said, it helps us see inside people like Charlie.

(17) A: I think the author wanted us to think that more. Maybe it wasn't natural, and that's bad, but the author, I don't know, is, more wants us not to think they're broken. What do you think?

(18) A: I agree. At the end of the book, I thought that a lot more than being mad about the experiment. If he died from that experiment, then it'd be different, but he didn't.

(19) B: OK.

QUESTIONS	NOTES FOR FEEDBACK
How well did the students build up each idea and follow the prompt?	19 turns was solid, built up both ideas, followed prompt well.
How well did they use examples from the text? Did they explain the evidence?	They supported the idea with examples from the text. Student B even used a personal example in line 12.
How well did they evaluate and compare the evidence on both sides?	They seemed to honestly struggle, in a good way, to come up with a decision, but they could have used criteria and explained their choice better in the end.
How hard did they try to explain their thoughts to one another?	Average length of turns was longer than average; plenty of rich language that focused on the content of the prompt.
How much or how well did they use academic thinking?	Interpretation: abstract ideas such as science helping people to be "better," the process not being natural, and people being "broken."

Table 5.3 Sample peer assessment tool

Inquiry-Based Improvement of Conversations

Inquiry-based improvement (similar to action research) means that you focus on a major instructional challenge or a question and try to experiment with different strategies to see whether they make a positive difference. In our case, based on evidence that you gather, you reflect on how to best improve student conversations. This can be done alone or, even better, in a small group of other teachers (e.g., professional learning communities [PLCs]).

One of the biggest challenges that emerges in my work with teachers is assessing all the conversations that happen in their lessons—which is, of course, impossible. Therefore, we need to be strategic, selective, and creative to effectively assess and learn from conversations. Here are some strategies:

- Creating a priority list that helps you observe the students you are more concerned about. You can also prioritize what you are looking for from the lists of features and dimensions in the beginning of this chapter (e.g., language, conversation skills, content understandings, thinking skills).
- Creating a schedule of observations over three weeks or so in order to observe complete conversations for every student in the class.

- Using recordings (on phones, tablets, computers) and strategically sampling and analyzing the recorded conversations.

Another challenge is figuring out what to *do* with the information you get from conversations. For example, you might have recorded and listened to several days of conversations in your fifth-grade classroom. Student conversations were extremely varied, with a wide range of strengths and areas to work on. How should you use this information to help design your next instruction steps? It helps to train your ears and eyes to look for patterns in the data and for themes that emerge, as a qualitative researcher might do. Often you will notice strengths and weaknesses in conversation skills, content understandings, use of thinking skills, and turn-taking. This skill takes time and practice with a lot of student conversations. The advantage, though, is that after a while you can observe several conversations in a day and get a strong feel for what the class needs next.

Practice Looking for Patterns

In the three fifth-grade conversations that follow, the students, in pairs, responded to the same prompt at the same time during a lesson. Imagine you are the teacher and analyze the three sample conversations for salient patterns, using the tool in Table 5.4 (cover the right-hand column) to focus your analysis and reflection. Students had engaged in a classroom discussion on the poem and etching by Paul Revere called the "Bloody Massacre on King Street" and were asked to talk about why he created them and what their impact might have been.

Conversation 1

(1)	A:	Why do you think Revere did this picture?
(2)	B:	I think to get people mad.
(3)	A:	What do you mean?
(4)	B:	He called it the "Bloody Massacre on King Street." But like only five people were killed.
(5)	A:	So?
(6)	B:	A massacre means lots of people die, like all over the place.
(7)	A:	But look at the picture.
(8)	B:	Yeah, look. How many dying people on the ground do you see?
(9)	A:	Three on the ground and two being carried.

(10) B: So, five, right? So that's right, but it looks like it was a lot more by looking at the soldiers. They're still shooting.

(11) A: And did Ms. L say that the colonists started it?

(12) B: It doesn't look it in the picture. So, Revere was kind of a liar, right?

(13) A: Yeah, but why lie?

(14) B: I don't think all the colonists wanted to fight. Especially the rich ones and ones with good jobs.

(15) A: OK. So it wasn't just saying what happened.

(16) B: Maybe it was a way to scare more people to think that more massacres would happen.

(17) A: I'd be scared if I saw this.

Conversation 2

(1) C: The soldiers look really mad.

(2) D: I think they're mad at the colonists.

(3) C: But they started it.

(4) D: Who?

(5) C: Colonists.

(6) D: Yeah, but the English were all over the city, the soldiers and guns. I wouldn't want that.

(7) C: And they were makin' them pay lots of taxes.

(8) D: What for?

(9) C: Prob'ly to pay for the soldiers.

(10) D: I see why they were mad.

(11) C: Why?

(12) D: They didn't want soldiers all around, like babysitters. They wanted to be on their own.

(13) C: So Revere made the picture have mean soldiers/

(14) D: /Yeah, to get everybody madder at them.

(15) C: I agree. Is that enough?

Conversation 3

(1)	E:	His poem it talks about blood and death a lot. Like here, "Thy hallow'd walks besmear'd with guiltless gore" and "Like fierce barbarians grinning o'er their prey, Approve the carnage and enjoy the day." Do you think it was like that? I don't. I don't think the soldiers thought that.
(2)	F:	Yeah, I think he's makin' up stuff to make it sound worse than it was. To make them like really evil.
(3)	E:	I think it made people more mad at them.
(4)	F:	But he just made up stuff. It's not right.
(5)	E:	He didn't make up the people killed by soldiers.
(6)	F:	Yeah, but he added stuff to it and called it a massacre. And like, he used it to get people mad. Look at the painting and the poem.
(7)	E:	So, was it right if it helped get us free?
(8)	F:	What do you mean?
(9)	E:	So maybe these things made enough people mad to fight the English.
(10)	F:	I don't know.

QUESTIONS	PATTERNS (+ AND –)
How well did the two students build up each idea and follow the prompt?	All three did some good building; they all built up ideas related to bias and propaganda.
How well did they clarify and prompt for clarification (with emphasis on cause-and-effect thinking)?	They asked a lot of helpful clarify questions, but they could have asked more cause-and-effect questions that might have led them to stronger ideas of what the impact was (the last part of the prompt).
How well did they use evidence from different sources, including primary sources?	They supported the idea with examples from primary sources, but each conversation only zoomed in on one or two evidences; they all need more evidence from the two sources.

Table 5.4 Sample assessment tool for noticing patterns in student conversations

Protocol for Analyzing Conversations

This protocol can help you analyze the learning evidence of multiple students in conversations, similar to the activity you just did. Each stage has guiding questions, suggested notes, and even teacher sentence starters to help spark your thinking and discussion, which are helpful if you are using this with others. You look for trends and patterns across the group of students. If you are in a learning community or grade-level group, you all can then suggest strategies to overcome challenges that you identify. Then you all meet again and bring in new evidence (notes, recordings, writing, etc.) to notice if and how the new instruction has influenced student learning.

I.   **Choose an Inquiry Question:** This question format can be *How can I improve (some aspect of student conversations), evidenced by (one or more types of evidence), by (using a certain teaching strategy or approach)?*

II. **Clarify Expectations:** What learning do I want/expect students' conversations to show? Starters: *I assume . . . I expect to see . . . I wonder . . . Some possibilities for learning that this data show are . . .*

III. **Observe Patterns and Trends:** What are the general trends observed? (Just the facts) Starters: *I observe that . . . Some patterns/trends that I notice . . . I counted . . . The percentage of . . . I'm surprised that I see . . .* (Avoid inferential terms such as *Because . . . Therefore . . . It seems . . . However . . .*)

IV. **Make Interpretations:** What can we interpret and infer about student learning from the evidence and data? Starters: *I believe the evidence suggests ___ because . . . Perhaps ___ is causing the pattern of . . . I think the students need . . .*

V.   **Ask Questions About the Data:** Usually, questions arise related to interpretations, such as *Why did these students do this? What can I do still to improve in this area? Is this evidence consistent and significant enough to change how I teach?*

VI. **Plan Solutions:** What are the implications for instruction and assessment? Starters: *We could try . . . because . . . This strategy or assessment would be most effective for this group . . . because . . .*

VII. **Plan What to Do and What to Bring for the Next Meeting:** Decide
which artifacts, evidence, and information will be most helpful for
answering the inquiry question in the next meeting. This also helps
you focus on what to do in the classroom that will generate the needed
evidence. Ask, *What are we going to bring to analyze in the next
collaboration? How will we teach and assess to get this evidence?* It is very
helpful to think like researchers at this point: *How can we organize what
we do and gather to get the most out of our work in answering our question?*
Possible formats are (a) all of us teaching the same way and assessing the
same way, (b) using different teaching strategies and bringing in the same
assessment, and (c) bringing different types of assessments for the same
teaching practice. Finally, ask, *What else will we do before the next meeting
to improve in this area and help answer our question (e.g., read books and
articles, attend trainings, observe peer lessons, have someone model a
practice in a classroom)?*

Diagnostic and Summative Assessments of Conversations

Most of this chapter has focused on formative assessment of student
conversations. Whereas formative assessment is ongoing throughout the year,
diagnostic assessments are used at the beginning of the year or semester, and
summative assessments are end-of-semester and end-of-year assessments,
more or less. You might give a diagnostic version of an assessment to see what
students already do proficiently and what they need to work on. You can also tell
students that at the end of the semester and year you will observe (or record)
a conversation that you and they will evaluate in a more summative way (with
some form of rubric). Let them know that their many conversations during the
year will be practice opportunities that prepare them for their final assessments.

Summative assessment of conversations gives students a big goal to shoot
for as they talk with others and work on their skills during the semester or year.
A teacher can pose a challenge such as *At the end of the semester, I'll record a
conversation between you and a partner about a topic that we just studied. I will
expect to hear effective use of conversation skills, academic language, thinking, and
so on.* With these objectives in mind, students have more purpose for practicing
these skills during the term. You can use one of the formative tools that you
designed or a more robust summative tool to guide the practice conversations
during the year and to assess the final conversations.

With respect to the types of conversation to use, I recommend some kind of argumentation, because it requires students to build up at least two ideas, not just one, and there is some competition between ideas, which tends to be more engaging. Even if students aren't able to deeply evaluate and compare the evidence used to build up the two sides, they usually can have solid enough conversations to show you what you want to know. The conversations also offer windows into students' content learning, speaking, listening, thinking, and nonverbal communication skills.

Write-Converse-Write Protocol

This assessment activity, developed by the Understanding Language team at Stanford University, consists of students doing a written pre-assessment, conversing with another student, and then doing a written post-assessment. This format is flexible, although if you do any comparison, whether with other teachers, over time, or between groups of students, try to keep what you ask students to do consistent.

The foundational format is WCW: Write (pre-assessment), Converse in pairs, and then Write again (post-assessment). The reason for this "sandwich" is to isolate and analyze the influence of the conversation between the two writing steps. Even though the writing shows only indirect evidence of conversations, it can be more easily collected and analyzed than trying to record all student conversations and listen to them all. Note that if you do too many different things between the pre-assessment and post-assessment (e.g., reading, oral language, video, pair-share), then you won't know what influenced the differences in the pre-assessment and post-assessment, so try to use just conversation in the middle of the process.

You get to see different things in the WCW format, such as

- conversation skills and content knowledge,
- writing skills and content knowledge,
- differences between the two writing samples and
- ways in which the conversation likely influenced the differences between the pre-assessments and post-assessments.

And if you gather conversation data in this way over time, you can record the improvement of conversations for one or more students during the year. You can also analyze the post-writing content learning and language development over time. Moreover, the WCW and its variants are not just assessments; they are also instructional in that students can learn from the conversations and gain needed writing practice.

Here is the procedure:

1. **Generate a prompt**. I recommend an argument-based prompt to promote longer and deeper conversations, but it's not necessary.

2. **(W) Have students respond in writing to the prompt**, letting them know that they will converse about their initial ideas with another student before writing about it again. Remind them to build up one or more ideas by clarifying and supporting with evidence, examples, and reasoning. If it's an argument-based prompt, remind them to build up both ideas as much as possible and then decide which idea is stronger.

3. **Gather their prewrites** with their names on them.

4. **(C) Pair them up and ask them to have a conversation with their partner**, using the prompt. Again, remind them to build up one or more ideas by clarifying and supporting with evidence, examples, and reasoning; and if it's an argument-based conversation, remind them to build up both ideas as much as possible and then decide which idea is stronger. Audio- or video-record this conversation.

5. **(W) Have students answer the prompt again in writing** (the post-assessment) without looking at the pre-assessment. Once more, remind them to build up one or more ideas by clarifying and supporting with evidence, examples, and reasoning, and if it's an argument-based prompt, remind them to build up both ideas as much as possible and then decide which idea is stronger. Try to give them roughly the same amount of time as they had for the prewrite. Gather these postwrites with names on them and match them to their prewrites. Optionally, have students highlight the information and ideas they got from the conversation in this postwrite.

6. **Use the tool below to analyze the differences between the prewrites and postwrites**. (You could also start by analyzing the conversation.) Watch or listen to the conversation, using the middle column of Table 5.5. Look for areas changed in the writing that are evident in the conversation.

In some cases, you might want to add activities before the pre-assessment to make the process more instructional. One could, for example, have two pair-shares (S), as in a Stronger-Clearer activity, before the prewriting, which would be SSWCW. Others could include Reading an article first, which would be RWCW. You could even have two conversations, one before and one after writing, which would be a CWC. Others could be CRC, CSC, CV(video)C, or even CTC, in which case the middle stage would be Teaching (modeling, practice, scaffolding) of a conversation skill or content. And finally, you could have ECE, in which the E is evidence such as a product, painting, or piece of music.

WCW Analysis Tool

You can use this tool or some variation that aligns with your current tools for assessing writing and conversation (see Table 5.5). The first six rows are used to rate and compare across pre-writing, post-writing, and the conversation in between, and there are three additional features to look at for the conversation. You can use 0, 1, 2 for *Not evident, Somewhat evident,* and *Evident* or other codes. Even more helpful are notes that you take.

STAGE	FEATURES IDEA(S)	RATINGS/NOTES
Prewrite, Conversation, and Postwrite	**Pose one or more relevant and buildable idea(s)**	
	Support idea(s) with evidence, examples, explanations (accurate content)	
	Clarify idea(s) and terms (if needed)	
	Disciplinary thinking (cause-effect, interpret, perspective, bias, analyze . . .)	
	Language use (vocabulary, grammar, organization)	
	If it's an **argument: evaluate and compare ideas** to choose strongest/heaviest side	
Conversation	**Build on one another's turns** and turn-taking	
	Value each other's ideas	
	Nonverbal communication	

Table 5.5 Sample Write-Converse-Write assessment tool

Sample WCW

Here is a sample WCW from a fourth-grade science class. The prompt was, *Pose a theory that explains how turtles came to have shells.*

Prewrite (Student A)

Turtles came to have shells because they wanted to not get eaten by cats and other things.

Converse

(1)	A:	So, I get that turtles have shells to protect them, but how did it start?
(2)	B:	It helps them live when like a big animal wants to eat 'em.
(3)	A:	I know, but I mean like how did the shell start?
(4)	B:	Oh. I don't know. Maybe it was a lizard before, and those things on their skin/
(5)	A:	/Scales?
(6)	B:	Yeah, they got bigger. The scales.
(7)	A:	Why?
(8)	B:	I don't know.
(9)	A:	But not just one lizard, right? Mr. S said that one is born a little different and that helped it. Like you said, maybe some had bigger scales.
(10)	B:	So, they lived better than the others with small scales. Maybe it was harder for like cats to eat them.
(11)	A:	Then it had babies with big scales. And they got bigger//
(12)	B:	//And they got bigger and stuck together, like turtles now.
(13)	A:	That's crazy.

Postwrite (Student A)

Turtles came to have shells because a long time ago they didn't have them. They were like lizards, maybe. And some were born different with bigger scales that helped them not get eaten. And they had babies and keep on getting bigger scales. They stuck together to make the shell, and now they are really protecting them from cats and big animals.

The obvious differences between the prewriting and postwriting samples are content and quantity. Student A had a much more robust idea of what natural selection was after the conversation. And you can see some expressions and terms used in the post-writing that A likely borrowed or simply picked up from the conversation. As for the conversation, it was very productive, zooming in on the key ideas of natural selection. Student B sparked the idea of a turtle being like a lizard a long time ago, and A added to the idea, especially in line 9. They asked clarifying questions and did some supporting (when referring to what Mr. S said), though they might have added a little more support from the book, pictures, or even what they knew about other animal adaptations. In this example, you can see a lot of differences that one conversation can make. Students can see these differences too, and this can inspire them to have better conversations over time.

Conversation Performance Assessment Task (Argument)

In this summative performance task, students engage in academic conversations based on argumentation and decision-making skills. Students are rated on how well they build, clarify, and support ideas, as well as how well they evaluate evidence, choose ideas, and collaborate throughout. You can put a rubric or rating tool together with the ideas in this chapter. You can do this at the beginning, middle, and end of the year to see their conversational growth. Here is the procedure:

1. Tell students that they will read the text(s) on _____. Tell them that after reading and a short whole-class discussion, they will be paired with another student at random to have a conversation to decide which side of the issue of _____ is stronger.

2. Students read the article or articles. They can take notes on the article or on a separate sheet of paper.

3. Lead a short five-minute class discussion that summarizes the different sides of the issue, with evidence and reasoning. Write these on a T-chart up front.

4. Tell them that they will have paired conversations and that you want them to use skills of clarifying ideas, supporting them with reasons and evidence, evaluating which idea is stronger (using criteria), and collaborating, to come up with a logical choice. Tell them they need to take turns and use appropriate language, and that it is OK to disagree near the end of the conversation, as long as they can both explain why they picked a certain side over the other. Often this will mean explaining how their values differed when they evaluated the weight of different evidences.

5. Pair students randomly (e.g., pulling two names at a time from a cup). If you know two students won't work well together, don't pair them. Remind students to take turns, clarify ideas, support ideas, and decide which idea is stronger regarding whether or not _____. They can look up at the board, at the texts, or at their notes, if needed. Do not assist in the conversations of students, unless it is necessary. Have them turn on the recording device, if you are using them.

6. After five minutes, stop the conversations.

7. Have students write down their final choice or decision and rationale for it.

Conversation Performance Assessment Task (Math)

The purpose of this performance task is to have students engage in academically productive conversations based on mathematical reasoning. Students will be rated on how well they clarify ideas, support ideas, and collaborate to build up ideas with appropriate turn-taking. The main goal of the conversation is not to come up with the right answer. Rather, it is to come up with several ways of solving it, clarifying them and allowing students to show their understanding of the principles and reasoning that the problem was supposed to teach. Here is the procedure:

1. Tell students that they will read a complex word problem. After reading, they will try to solve it by themselves. Remind students that understanding and clarity is the goal, not just the answer. (Some teachers even give the answer at the start.)

2. Have students read the problem and try to solve it.

3. Tell them that they will have paired conversations and that you want them to use skills of clarifying ideas and supporting them with solid mathematical reasoning. You can remind them that they should at least justify their procedures, but that you also want them to make claims and generalizations about how math works, with logical justification.

4. Pair students randomly (e.g., pulling two names at a time from a cup). If you know two students won't work well together, don't pair them. Have them turn on their recording devices, if you are using them.

5. Have students talk together to come up with at least two solution methods. They need to be able to clearly explain them to others and explain the connections between them (e.g., how an algorithm is represented by a visual and vice versa). Remind students to take turns, clarify, and justify. They can look up at the board, at other problems, or at their notes, if needed.

6. After five minutes, have them stop their conversations.

7. Have students write down their final explanation of the math that they were supposed to learn and how the problem was an example of how math works. This can also serve as a formative assessment to see the thinking and language of students you could not observe during the activity.

Teacher Support for Conversations

Finally, I thought it would be helpful to include a short list of teacher practices that come from this and previous chapters in this book. This is just an initial list that you can use, add to, and edit to get you started on creating teacher self-assessment and observation tools.

How effectively do you as teacher . . .

- create engaging purposes and clear prompts for conversing?
- set up conversations so that each student has information, ideas, or opinions that partners don't know yet? (so that they can bridge information gaps.)
- provide language supports to help students communicate, as needed?
- provide sufficient modeling, scaffolding, and time for productive and extended talk?
- support a classroom environment in which students feel safe in sharing their ideas with others?
- help students value conversation as a way to learn and build relationships?
- choose, design, or adapt curriculum to leverage conversations for learning?
- observe conversations and respond to the strengths and needs that you see?

Conclusion

We will never have perfectly valid and reliable assessments for all conversations in school, but we must keep on assessing them as effectively as possible, for several reasons: (1) to see what students have learned and what they still need to learn, (2) to learn how to improve our communication with students, and (3) to provide feedback that we and our students can use to improve their conversation skills. Many teachers have commented that they have learned much more about student learning from observing their conversations than from quizzes and tests. Other teachers have said that conversation assessments are often so instructional that it is like getting two good things (learning and assessment) for the price of one activity.

Chapter 6

Cultivating Conversation Mindsets, Cultures, and Supports

*It takes a village to raise a child
who excels at conversing with others.*

This final chapter brings the ideas in the previous chapters together to help you set up doable action items to create thriving conversations in your setting(s). These action items need to work together to support the development of conversations across grade levels and disciplines. The action items fall within three overlapping dimensions: (1) conversation mindsets, (2) classroom cultures and practices, and (3) schoolwide systems and supports.

Conversation Mindsets

This first dimension operates at the level of the student. As you already know, the foundation of learning is not in the curriculum but in the student's mind. One component of this foundation is the student's beliefs, or mindsets, about how learning works. In our case, we are trying to improve, deepen, and develop students' mindsets for learning how to converse and how to learn by conversing. Here are several mindsets to nurture in students and some suggestions for doing so.

We learn best by building up ideas—and we try to build up each idea as much as possible.

It is vital to have students thinking thoughts such as "Learning means doing a range of things (reading, writing, thinking, talking, listening, watching, conversing) to build up meaningful ideas." This student mindset primarily comes from the influence of our teacher mindsets about learning, what we say and do, and the types of learning and assessment tasks that we have students engage in during lessons.

This building-ideas mindset, of course, means bucking the system in many settings. If you deal with educators who think that "sit and git and spit it back out" is the main way for students to learn (and show learning with test scores), you have an uphill battle. But in places that are open to having students converse, where they value student voices, and where they allow them to construct ideas, meaningful and lasting learning happens.

This mindset is foundational in many successful classrooms and is a cornerstone of conversation work. And yet, of the mindsets I'll be discussing, it's probably the hardest to foster. Common cultural forces such as social media, television, texting, and video games tend to encourage short answers and unformed ideas. And schooling in recent decades hasn't helped much. The forces of disjointed tests and mile-wide-inch-deep curriculums have not encouraged learning based on building ideas. When you read a bunch of short, disconnected texts and answer multiple-choice questions, you don't really get much practice in using lots of language and thinking in order to build up complex ideas in a discipline. Just ask most students what they think the theme of a short story is and you will often hear one-liners such as "It's about friendship," or, "Don't judge a book by its cover." And partners will respond with responses such as "Yeah. I agree. That's a good idea," or, "I disagree because I think it's about love." Interactions like these don't build up ideas.

But when students believe that they can and need to build up ideas with one another as much as possible, learning reaches a new level. Rather than speaking and listening at minimum or mediocre levels, students max out the building of each idea as they converse, listen, talk, read, and write.

To foster this mindset, you can emphasize building up ideas in a wide range of situations. During class discussions you can often ask, *Have we built up this idea as much as possible?* and we can encourage students to grow in this way of thinking. Encourage students to ask this question before they turn in their writing and whenever they read, talk, listen, or draw.

Throughout the year, you can evaluate the strength of this and other mindsets with quick-writes and surveys. You can directly ask them, *What are you learning? What ideas have you built up so far? What ideas are you currently building? How do you best learn? How do conversations help you learn?* and similar questions.

In an argument, it's better to choose a side after all sides are built up.

This mindset runs counter to how many students and adults think when engaged in argumentation. Often, well before students have objectively and completely built up all sides of an issue, they quickly form an opinion and try to back it up. They tend to stick to their guns and try to win at all costs, often with skewed reasoning and limited evidence. Do you know any adults who do this? OK, most of us do this at times. But we and our students can improve. We can teach students to hide or hold their opinions until the end or, even better, not to solidify their opinions before all ideas have been built up as much as possible.

A related habit is sticking to the mantra *Build up the first idea first*. So, even if in the back of your mind you vehemently oppose the first idea, you clarify and share as much as you can with your partner (who may also oppose it) to build up the first idea first. This provides both students with a more objective chance to decide which idea is stronger, because they have given every idea a full process of thinking. It also takes away the stress of trying to win. Students might still stick to their original opinions, but those opinions become more informed because students have built them up and weighed them against a fully formed opponent in a fairer contest.

To foster this mindset, you can provide a range of visual scaffolds, one of which is the model in Figure 6.2, which shows a balance scale visual with the ideas to build up on both sides. You can also require students to use a certain number of cards for each side when they use the idea-building cards, as described in Chapter 2. You can get students into the habit of asking one another and themselves, "Are the idea and its components as clear as they can be?" "Are there any other evidences, examples, or reasons that would make this idea stronger?" They will often need to be encouraged to build up their ideas more than they think is needed.

I respect, value, and learn from others.

Many students have the mindset that all learning comes from listening to the teacher or from reading texts. This kind of learning tends to be focused on facts and isolated skills (such as problem solving in math). We need to foster the mindset that (a) they can learn a lot from interacting with peers and (b) this learning also includes the development of social skills, relationships, language, and thinking skills (things beyond just information). This means that we want students to value the language used by others, even if there are grammatical mistakes or vocabulary errors. This means valuing the ideas of others in the class, even if at first the ideas don't seem relevant, useful, or correct. And this means valuing the different ways in which others think. The more that students (and all of us) learn how other humans think about life, the world, and academic topics, the better.

The companion mindset for this one, which is a result of respecting and valuing, is that students feel safe sharing their ideas with others. This "I feel safe sharing whatever I am thinking" belief is vital, especially for students who typically don't talk much in class. When they feel valued and respected, they are less afraid to share, and their wonderful ideas get added to the collective learning in the class.

To foster this mindset, you can show model conversations that demonstrate good valuing of ideas, as well as non-model conversations that show non-valuing and disrespect. When showing the non-valuing examples, ask students how they think the student at the receiving end of the non-valuing feels. Have the class help you make a poster of the ways in which they can respond to partners to show how they value what is being said. And as you observe conversations, you should reinforce the valuing that students do as much as possible.

Conversations are powerful opportunities for me (us) to shape and own what I (we) learn.

This mindset is focused on agency, the feeling that students have some control over what and how they are learning. We want them to think,

- "I feel more like a learner when I talk about academic topics with others."
- "I feel more confident about my ideas because I talk about them."
- "I like to create ideas with others as we talk."
- "When I talk, I have the freedom to think about and express my ideas in ways that I think are most effective."
- "I like to add my own information and personal touches to the ideas, and conversations let me do this."

For the many students who need to catch up to their peers, thinking thoughts such as these can make them much more motivated to go beyond the bare minimum in their thinking and conversing.

To foster this mindset, remind students of the value of using their own background knowledge and creativity to co-build ideas with others. Remind them that ideas will look different, and that's OK. You can say things such as

"Wow! I have never seen someone approach a problem in that way. How creative is that?" Encourage peers to respond similarly. And have students exhibit their ideas in settings such as school newspapers, podcasts, and science fairs, where they feel they are adding to the learning of others. The more that students feel that their unique thinking and ideas are helping and teaching others in the world, the more their confidence and sense of ownership flourishes.

And at the teacher level, many of us need to raise our own expectations for how well students can work together to build ideas and make logical decisions in conversations. Teachers have told me, "They can't really talk with each other about academic topics yet." Yes, they can. Even if they get off to a rocky and slow start, students can and *must* engage in conversations every day in school. We want students to be thinking, "My teachers and others at the school expect me to do great things and build up important ideas with others. And they expect me to have conversations that do this."

I belong in this academic setting.

One of the most important human desires, especially in young people, is to belong in a setting and in a group. Many students feel like they don't belong in school or can't contribute or learn alongside other students in class. We can counter this by encouraging a sense of belonging in every student during conversations.

One of the things that conversations can provide is daily connection with other students. Imagine spending five hours next to classmates with very little eye contact or very few words exchanged. (Actually, try shadowing students for a day and you will likely observe this.) In this situation, students might feel that they are not interesting, not friendly, not worthy of friendship, or worse. Conversations and other face-to-face communication, even awkward exchanges, can and do reduce such feelings. I have talked to many students who said that they have many more friends and like school more because the teacher has them talk to one another on a regular basis.

To foster this mindset, you can have certain routines in place for students who might not feel like they belong or for other students who might feel out of place, not as smart, or not as good at being a student as their peers. One teacher I know has students volunteer to be a long-term welcoming committee. They help students, in class and out of class, to learn the ropes and feel like they belong—in the class, in the school, and even in the country, if they have immigrated.

Classroom Culture and Practices

Like a tree planted in bad soil or a large skyscraper constructed on a weak foundation, deep learning through conversation won't happen without a classroom culture that supports, nourishes, and values communication. Culture includes values, beliefs, mindsets, and how a group of people do things together.

The most effective way to foster conversational culture is to weave conversations and other interaction activities into the fabric of daily teaching. A lot of research on classroom culture and motivation is summed up by several essential elements, which I have put into the following suggestions.

Improve Pairing and Grouping

I am often asked, "Should I pair students strategically or randomly?" and as you might guess, my answer is *yes*. Students can benefit from talking with certain others at certain times, and they can benefit from random pairings, just like they will experience in later schooling and in real life. The downside of strategic pairing is the time it takes to set up the pairs. The upside is that more language and content might be used and built between certain students. Here are some specific ways to improve pairing and grouping:

- Pair students for several weeks to have continuing conversations during which they can keep building up ideas.
- Identify certain students who you know are good at modeling good conversation behaviors and who can help less conversational students talk more. Meet with these students at times and ask them to be open to meeting and talking with a range of others in the class. If they are heavy talkers, remind them to listen and value the ideas of partners.
- Use conversation lines (and inner-outer circles) to help students change partners during activities in which they talk to more than one partner (e.g., Stronger and Clearer). You can also strategically place certain students to purposefully talk with (or not talk with) certain others.
- Use clock partners, in which students sign up for talking with four (or more) other partners at certain times during the day or week. You might say, "OK, now meet with your nine o'clock partner, and here is the prompt." You can help set up the partnerships.

- Use pairs more often during whole-class presentations such as modeling, lectures, and videos. Every few minutes or so, most brains start to wander during this kind of instruction. Pair work can prevent this wandering by pushing students into talking about the content.

Improve the Quantity and Quality of Pair-Shares

Pair-shares, think-pair-shares, and turn-and-talks are short interactions in which students pair up and share their responses to a teacher prompt with each other. They are great opportunities to practice conversation skills, and sometimes the pair-shares become conversations. Usually, though, one student shares first and then the other shares. After pair time, ask some students to share with the class what their partners said or what new idea they were able to put together based on sharing and listening. This gives them more incentive to listen during the share, and publicly validates what their partner said.

Even though pair-shares have been used for decades, some lessons could use more of them. Some teachers use a 5-2 rule, which means for every five minutes of listening (e.g., to the teacher) or reading, students do something to process the information, such as a pair-share. So be aware of how often students get to share and process what they are learning. Try adding at least one or two more pair-shares per lesson, and see how it goes. And as often as possible, give students time to think before they share. This think time can be very productive.

To improve the quality of pair-shares, students can benefit from making several enhancements:

- **Give a purpose for the pair-share that goes beyond it**. Some students won't put much effort into the pair-share if they don't really see the value of it. If they think that it's just a chance for you to take a break (as if you ever get breaks) or watch them exchange answers, the bare minimum will prevail. But if students see the information they get from their partners as useful, or they realize that it helps them to put their evolving ideas into words for a partner, then you will get more learning.
- **Have one partner share first** (e.g., student A) **for a certain amount of time**. Ask them to try to fill the time (rather than just saying half a sentence and telling the partner, "Your turn"). If A says very little, B can help by asking questions or providing idea seeds with "What about … ?" Then give time for B. And in the next pair-share, have student B start.

- **Have listeners ask the talker to clarify and support**. Instead of just nodding their heads when listening, have listeners pick out something from the talker's message that could use some clarification, such as an abstract idea or key term. Also, have listeners prompt for more and better support. You can even say, "When you are the listener, ask one clarify or support question to the talker."
- **Make sure that both students in a pair have different information to share** (i.e., that there is an information gap to cross). If they have the same information, there is little need to talk or listen. In some cases, this different information comes from differing background knowledge or perspectives, texts that each student has read, or even information on cards that you provide to students. You can also create two different questions for the share—one for each student—so they can't say things such as "Ditto" or "I agree."
- **Have students engage in two or three pair-shares in a row**. (This is the foundation for Stronger and Clearer activities, described in Chapter 3.) The first pair-share for many students is just an oral draft, and often students start with a very basic idea. But with multiple pair-shares, students can ask one another clarify and support questions, and they can practice what they are saying a couple of times, borrowing from previous partners. Students push and are pushed to improve ideas. A variation of this is the think-pair-square: after pairs are done sharing with each other, they turn to another pair to share what they heard from their partners. This gives students a chance to share with three people instead of the entire class. It is also a good way to create groups of four for other activities.
- **Encourage students to improve their pair-shares in various ways**, with ideas from Table 6.1.
- **Vary the structure**. Insert various reading and writing components: think-write-pair-share (TWPS); think-pair-write-share (TPWS); read-pair-share (RPS); and others such as RWPS, TWRPS, TRWPWS, TWRWPSW, and so on. Try them out and see what works best for your students.

AS A TALKER . . .	AS A LISTENER . . .
Start with the main idea or topic sentence. This might be an opinion, claim, hypothesis, conjecture, process, interpretation, etc.	Face the partner, show interest, and listen actively. You can take notes but only one or two words during listening in order to minimize looking down and halting the talker's flow.
After saying your topic sentence (e.g., an opinion), think about any words that you just used that might need clearing up in the listener's mind. They might ask you, but it is better to clarify before they ask you.	Don't interrupt. Give your partner time and space to think, start over, etc. If you think that clarification would help, prompt the partner *(Do you mean that . . . ? Why do you think that? Where does it say that? Did you get that from a website? So you are saying that . . .).*
Give evidence from the book, class discussions, or your own life. (Evidence can also clarify ideas.)	Remember what your partner says so you can share it out or use it for another task (but don't take long notes during talking).

Table 6.1 Ways to improve pair-shares as talkers and as listeners

Talk About How to Have Effective Conversations

You should also have discussions and minilessons in which you talk about how to have effective conversations. These are *meta-conversations* because you talk about how to have the most productive conversations possible, in and out of school. You can talk about the power of conversations for learning in school along with their importance for friendships, relationships, and interacting with others in the working world.

I recommend analyzing model and non-model conversations to see what the model conversations are doing well (clarifying, supporting, evaluating, building, valuing) and what the non-model conversations are not doing well. You can also hold live model conversations that you set up between two students (prepare them beforehand) or between you and a student. These discussions can be a way to highlight the importance of working together to achieve complex learning tasks and to build up important ideas in a discipline.

Emphasize that during the year students will gradually take more control of their conversations and rely less on you. Remind them that clarifying, supporting, and evaluating are two-way skills, which means that students need to know when and how to prompt partners to do these things, and they need to know how to respond when partners prompt for them.

In the following meta-conversation in fifth-grade social studies, the teacher wanted to highlight the importance of getting evidence from different perspectives. The non-model conversation on the screen focused on how the Spaniards were able to maintain control over the Aztecs after the conquest. The teacher started by having students take the two roles of the students in the non-model conversation. Then she had them pair up and asked, *How could this conversation be better?* After the pair-share, she asked them to share their thoughts in the whole-class conversation.

(1)	A:	They could talk more. Their answers were short.
(2)	B:	And David shared, like, just an opinion and not evidence.
(3)	T:	Great. Any others? Remember the importance of learning about all perspectives.
(4)	C:	Well, I think there was lots of stuff from the Spaniards, like their evidence, but not much from the Aztecs.
(5)	T:	Do others agree? Should there be more evidence from the Aztec perspective? How would it help?
(6)	D:	You can't just have one side's opinion. We need the other side.
(7)	T:	Why?
(8)	B:	Cuz it's not fair. You can't just listen to one side.
(9)	T:	Why?
(10)	E:	We gotta learn about all sides and all people, like what they thought.
(11)	A:	And what's that saying we learned last month? "History is written by . . ."
(12)	F:	The winners?
(13)	T:	Yes, so how does that relate to our discussions?
(14)	G:	I think we gotta, we gotta get the truth, like cuz we learned that the losers don't write as much. Or they get their writings and art all burned up.
(15)	T:	So? Wait. Tell a partner. Why should we work hard to find out what the losers of wars and victims of conquests thought?

Fortify Your Activities with Conversations and Their Skills

As you have already seen aplenty in this book, we can and should modify much of what we do in class to help students build their conversation skills. This can mean adding conversations to existing activities. For example, you might stop a video halfway through and have students talk about a hypothesis they have formed while watching. You can also push students to clarify and support ideas whenever they are sharing thoughts with one another. In the middle of writing an essay, for example, have students read their draft to a partner and have a conversation about what they are trying to communicate and the language they are using. (For example, *Why are you using that language to describe the counterclaim? Did you use this sentence fragment to make a point?*). Strive to weave the skills of building ideas, clarifying, and supporting into as many activities and discussions as possible.

You have already seen quite a few modifications to learning activities in this book (e.g., modified jigsaws, whole-class discussions, Socratic seminars). Here are some additional insights that you can use for adapting other familiar activities. But first, here is an idea to reflect on: *If a learning activity doesn't build up one or more ideas in some way, or if you can't adjust it somewhat easily to help your students build up ideas, then consider removing it from your school year.* I know that's a strong statement, but there are enough idea-building activities to fill the little time that we have with our students, and they will be much better off as a result. In fact, every activity in which students meaningfully speak or listen can be an opportunity to develop conversation skills that build ideas and improve conversation abilities.

Here is a set of features that you can use to strengthen, conversationally, what you already do. Feel free to modify it. Learning activities can often have more and better opportunities to allow students to

- choose what they want to converse about;
- clarify ideas, importance, values, and feelings;
- support ideas with evidence, examples, and reasoning;
- evaluate evidence;
- use disciplinary thinking skills in conversation with others;
- talk about their writing and other products that show their learning;
- talk about what they are reading;
- build up ideas that will keep building for years to come.

Table 6.2 has suggestions for ways to use these features to make common activities more conversational in your lessons.

ACTIVITIES	CONVERSATIONAL ADJUSTMENTS
Read and answer questions	Have students converse about their varying answers to more conversation-worthy question(s). Make sure the questions help students build up ideas, not just test their comprehension. Have them question the questioner: *Why did the writer or teacher ask me this question?*
Create a group poster	Make sure the poster has a purpose beyond just getting points (e.g., it helps others build up a big idea). Have students meet in pairs before and during the poster creation to talk about their varying ideas for representing the ideas and why. Students ask each other to clarify and support ideas related to the poster.
Whole-class discussion and note taking	Have frequent pair-shares in which listeners prompt for clarification and support to help the talker build up the idea. Use a Building Ideas Visual (see Chapter 2) for note taking during the discussion. Ask students to prompt their peers with prompts that they think you would ask, or say, *What would be a good response to Elisa's comment?*
Take a side (or four corners)	After students have built up both (all) sides, they stand up and choose a side (or a corner). They then turn to a partner on that side and describe the strongest evidence used to build up that side (why they chose it). You can have several students in the middle and have the two sides (or four corners) try to convince them to join their side (see Take a Side in Chapter 3). They can start with acknowledging the evidence on the other side: "Even though we realize that . . . , we argue that the evidence of . . . is stronger and . . ."
Gallery walk	Have students who are in each group making a poster practice what they will say, before you pick which one. They can practice in two successive pair-shares with different partners (A and B, C and D, then A and C, B and D) in which they prompt for clarifying and supporting of the main idea. Then call on one person, let's say D, to stay at the group's poster and present. Then as D presents the poster to others who circle around, have listeners ask clarify, support, and (if D is arguing for one side of an issue) evaluation questions. (*What criteria did you use? Why?*) Also give listeners a purpose for listening—the entire activity should help all students build up important ideas.
Watch a video	Stop the video at times to have students engage in mini-conversations about a key clarification or piece of evidence. Have students fill in a Building Ideas Visual (see Chapter 2) or Argument Balance Scale (see Chapter 3) during the video (stop at times to allow for more thinking and writing time). Then have students meet with other students to compare and fill in any bricks that they didn't record.

Table 6.2 Sample conversational adjustments for common classroom activities

Let Students Engage in Conversations

In some classrooms, I have observed lessons in which teachers over-structured students' conversations with lots of sentence frames, interruptions, and even memorized dialogues. Even though you have seen sentence starters in this book, use them sparingly and strategically, and take them away as soon as possible. Provide some modeling before conversation time and then let students productively push one another and themselves in real conversations. These might be messy, imperfect, too short, too long, off topic, or strange, but over time they will improve. Be patient. This dedicated conversation practice will help them rack up the many hours that they need to become experts in conversing and interacting with others.

Continue to remind students that the focus of conversations should be on building ideas. Students will find thousands of different ways to use words, images, memories, and actions to build ideas as they converse with others. This means you need to provide just enough materials and structure to (a) get students started and (b) keep them building.

Train Students to Coach Each Other in Conversations

This action item is really a collection of activities that all focus on helping students become expert enough at conversations to coach their peers. In these activities, one student becomes an observer-coach who listens to a conversation between two peers and helps them at times to deepen and extend their conversation. As you can imagine, this process also builds conversational expertise along the way, helping the observer-coaches have better conversations when it's their turn to talk. The following three activities include ways to use observer-coaches.

Rotating Mini-Jigsaw Triads

The name of this activity says most of what you need to know. This activity allows students to converse and coach each other on their conversations within the same activity. And it allows them to reinforce thinking skills and content because each student engages in two conversations.

1. Divide the text up into six parts to read.

2. Put students in triads (A, B, and C). A reads part one and B reads part two.

3. A and B respond to a prompt for the first two parts and start a conversation, while C observes and coaches them. Especially when A and B get stuck, stop, or need to clarify, C helps by prompting A, B, or both to do something conversationally helpful. C tries not to become an equal third partner, but C doesn't have to be silent (just like a basketball coach doesn't usually scrimmage the whole time or check in to play during a real game).

4. Students rotate roles: B and C read parts three and four, and A coaches them. Finally, A and C read parts five and six, and B coaches. The three prompts should connect and should help students build up a central idea from the text.

Here is an example from ninth-grade history. The texts were three short articles, split into two parts each, about the First Amendment and whether it protects hate speech. A and B were conversing, and C was the coach.

(1) C: OK, your prompt is *What is the First Amendment and why do you think we have it?*

(2) A: So, what is it?

(3) B: It's a rule that, it says it here, it protects free speech.

(4) A: OK, so why do we have it?

(5) C: Wait. You should probably clarify that.

(6) B: OK, what does *protect free speech* mean?

(7) A: I think it's like you can say what you think, and they don't arrest you.

(8) B: Even if they're wrong or evil?

(9) A: Yeah.

(10) B: So, what's next?

(12) C: An example of free speech might help here. Maybe from the article?

(13) A: I got one. A court case. They decided a person could say all kinds of bad names to others, call people racist names, but it was legal.

(14) B: That's just wrong.

(15) A: Yeah, I agree. Like on the news, I saw people with signs and bad words on them. They were really mad.

(16) B: I don't get it. *[Silence.]*

(17) C: What about the rest of the prompt?

(18) A: Why do we have it?

(19) B: In my section, it says it was put there cuz the first people wanted to be free and didn't want government tellin' 'em what to say.

(20) A: But I think it's wrong to call people names.

(21) B: Yeah. It's not right.

Notice how the student in the coach role helped to improve the conversation at key moments. These three students then switched roles and continued to build their ideas about what kinds of speech are protected by the First Amendment and why.

Silent Coaching Cards

Similar to the previous activity, this activity has a third person who listens to the conversation and coaches the partners. But in this case, the coach tries to be silent and let the two partners talk. Using various premade cards along with blank cards, the coach gives a card to one or both of the talkers to help improve and extend the conversation. Of course, if a card is unclear or the talkers need more explanation, the coach can talk. But the coach tries to avoid being a third partner (which is difficult to do for talkative students). The premade cards have suggestions, usually based on conversation skills, such as the ones in Table 6.3.

Ask your partner to clarify _____ (Why, How . . .)	Refer to the text	Ask for evidence or an example to support the idea	Keep building up the first idea
Paraphrase what your partner said	Agree on a definition of _____	Explain how and how well the evidence supports the idea	Stay focused on the conversation purpose or prompt
Encourage your partner to talk more (and give time)	Show you are listening with eyes, nods, posture, etc.	Pose an alternative idea and start to build it up	

Table 6.3 Examples of Silent Coaching Cards

You will need to model the use of the cards for several months so that students get the gist of how they work. The advantage of this activity is that you can, after the conversations are over, collect the cards and get a sense of how well the conversations are going and what you still need to work on. Here is a sample conversation in seventh-grade science during which a student-observer silently slipped support cards to students, as shown here.

(1)   A: So, why do squids have ink?

(2)   B: I think to hide.

(3)   A: What do you mean?

(4)   B: They hide in it.

(5)   A: OK . . .

(6)   C: Passes this silent coaching card to Student A

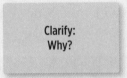

Clarify:
Why?

(7)   A: OK, so why do they hide in their ink?

(8)   B: When they get scared, like maybe a big fish comes after them.

(9)   A: OK, I think they got ink to . . . , they escape. Like the picture. They let it out; it makes a cloud so they, you know, can swim away.

(10)   B: Yeah . . .

(11)   C: Passes this silent coaching card to Student B

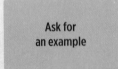

Ask for
an example

(12)   B: Can you give an example?

(13)   A: Yeah. Maybe like you said. A shark comes after it, but it makes a big cloud of ink, and that lets it swim away, cuz the shark gets confused.

(14)   B: Did you see that show on that really huge shark?

(15)   A: No.

(16)   B: It has teeth this big *[holding hands apart]*.

(17)   C: Puts this card between both students

Stay focused
on the prompt

Conversation Observer Visuals

These visual organizers are derived from several activities and suggestions in previous chapters (see Figures 6.1 and 6.2). As you can see, they emphasize the building of ideas. The observer can put in a letter code and a short note related to the code. If a student says, "For example, the main character gave her ticket to her brother," the observer could put "S gave ticket" in a brick. On the side, the observer could put notes on strengths and areas to improve, such as body language, valuing each other's ideas, equal amounts of speaking, and so forth. The observer then shares the notes with the conversers and they can work together to identify any areas to improve (e.g., more clarifying).

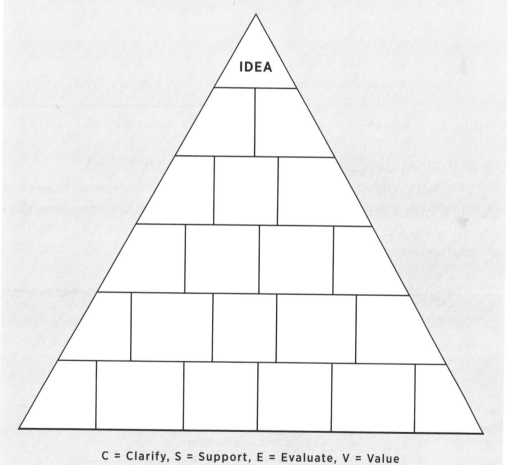

C = Clarify, S = Support, E = Evaluate, V = Value

Figure 6.1 Sample visual organizer for third observer notes (building an idea)

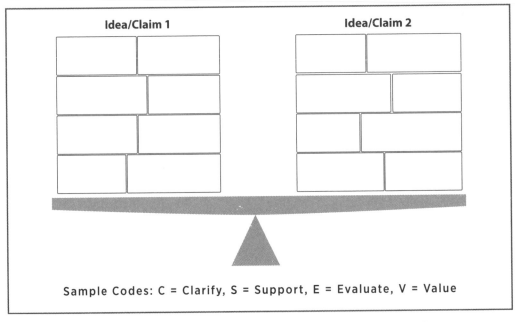

Sample Codes: C = Clarify, S = Support, E = Evaluate, V = Value

Figure 6.2 Sample visual organizer for third observer notes (argument)

Use an If-When-Can Chart for Troubleshooting Conversations

You can have students use a chart as in Table 6.4 below to address problems and issues that arise when doing conversation work. (The "You" at the top of the "You Can" column is for students.) When you notice frequent issues, put them in the left-hand column and, along with students, brainstorm things they can do to fix it.

IF . . . OR WHEN . . .	YOU CAN:
the conversation doesn't start well—or at all,	• say, "Let's understand (clarify, define) this . . . What we need to do is . . ." • ask, "What does . . . mean in this case/context/situation?" • say, "Let's scan through the text again and look for . . ." • say, "Let's take two different sides. Which one do you want?"
your partner offers a short response,	• ask for specific clarification. • ask a question (*I wonder why/how . . .*). • ask what a word or expression means. • ask for an example that supports it. • Ggive an example and ask whether your partner agrees.

IF . . . OR WHEN . . .	YOU CAN:
your partner offers a long and confusing response,	• paraphrase it and relate it to the conversation's purpose. • ask to clarify the most relevant part of the response. • ask for additional evidence or examples.
your partner shares a piece of evidence, without enough explanation	• ask how the evidence supports the idea. • ask how *well* the evidence supports the idea. • ask for additional evidence and examples: "What is the other evidence that might support your idea?" • compare and contrast it to similar opposing evidence: "I wonder if that is more supportive of the argument than . . ."
The first idea has been sufficiently built up with multiple examples from both partners,	• ask what the partner thinks is the most/least influential evidence. • recap (summarize) the building of the first idea. • pose an opposing idea. • play devil's advocate and argue against the idea just for thinking and communication practice. • ask, "What are different perspectives on this?"
you share an initial idea and get little response ("Yeah," "OK," "Uh-huh," "Hmm"),	• ask your partner what he or she thinks about the idea. • ask your partner for his or her evidence for the idea. • tell your partner to disagree so you can make the idea stronger. • ask, "Do we have enough evidence to argue this idea?"

Table 6.4 If-When-Can chart for troubleshooting conversations

Tailor Conversations to Different Stages of Learning

Conversations can and should differ, depending on the stages of learning in a lesson or unit. For initial conversations about a topic, for example, students will focus on different aspects of building up an idea than in middle or final stage conversations. You could have these three stages in one lesson, a week of lessons, or even at the unit level (e.g., three or four weeks of lessons).

While no two ideas will look exactly alike in the end, you should create a rough draft of some of the elements that you want to see and hear in your students' final ideas.

In initial stage conversations, which are early on in a lesson or unit, students focus on preparing to build up an idea. They talk about what they need to do, what they already know related to the idea to be built, what resources and steps they need to take, and how they plan to get the information.

In middle stage conversations, students have their main conversations for building up the idea. They talk to gain as much knowledge and evidence as possible, ideally with different partners, and they work on the best ways of communicating it all to others. They talk about the information they have been gathering, and the quality of evidence, and make any evaluations needed to compare competing sides in an argument to choose the best one. And they talk about how to clarify to others all they have done to build up (or choose) ideas.

In the final stage conversations, students talk about what they have built and how to most effectively communicate it to others. This could include conversing about how to create a visual, slide show, video, podcast, or combination of these. They might bring up any final missing "bricks" needed to complete their idea or engage in any final clarifications.

Schoolwide Systems and Supports

To change minds, develop practices, and sustain conversations in school, it is vital to have system-wide alignment, joint efforts, and large-scale buy-in on the part of teachers and administrators. I was talking with one teacher who told me that they were working extra hard to get most teachers on board with conversation work, and that they knew it would be a long-term project. Her goal was to reach a point where new teachers would ask about all the conversations going on in classes, and teachers and administrators would answer, "This is a cornerstone for how we do learning around here." Here are some action items that can help you foster that type of system in your setting.

Get Schoolwide Agreement on the Value of Conversations

If only a few teachers and leaders at a school think that conversations are valuable, it's an uphill battle. The shift to more conversational learning is a big and fragile one, and you need a critical mass of educators on board. For example, a student may do some great conversation work in grades three and four, but the fifth grade teacher might not see its value. A lot can be lost in a year, especially with respect to social and conversation skills.

So, if needed, read up on all the benefits, and present them to colleagues and leadership at the school. Many helpful resources are in the back of this book. If you can get into different classrooms, collaborate with teachers who agree to work on conversations with their students. Observe and video-record conversations, and collect writing samples and other products that directly result from conversations. Share this evidence at department meetings, staff meetings, and PLC meetings. Also share with leaders at all levels to get solid buy-in and support from them. This is especially needed for conversation work because many leaders are highly interested in reading and writing test scores, and they don't often see the connection between conversations and scores. Conversation-based learning seems like a risky shift that many are not ready to make without some heavy convincing. And some haven't yet seen (or looked for) the vital benefits of conversations, such as the growth of social skills, friendships, empathy, confidence, emotional intelligence, academic identity, and agency.

Make Conversations the Focus of Professional Learning Communities

Professional learning communities (PLCs) are groups of people in a similar job setting who meet regularly to improve how they do things. Often, PLCs consist of teachers of the same grade level or content area. They meet and bring in evidence of learning, such as student work or videos, to collaboratively learn how best to teach students. I usually recommend focusing on a certain topic for two or more semesters, or on an important question or problem. And, being biased toward the topics in this book, I often recommend focusing on improving students' conversation skills.

I encourage teachers to come up with a "backward planned" inquiry that starts from what they are trying to improve (e.g., one or more conversation skills), then considers the types of evidence they will use to see improvement or the lack thereof (e.g., video clips, notes, student self-assessments, writings connected to conversation work), and concludes with the teaching strategy they will introduce to try to create the improvement. As they bring in evidence and anecdotes of success and failure, teachers hone their knowledge and skills for meeting the unique conversation needs of their students. Many who are involved in PLCs argue that it is the most effective professional development they have participated in.

Schoolwide Agreement on Conversational Goals

Most standards don't zoom in enough on what students need to be able to do in conversations each year. It's up to us to work this out. After reading this book, you should have a better idea of what you want your students to do in conversations in your grade level and content areas. Equipped with this knowledge, listen to their conversations for several months, or even a year. In this time, you will become an expert in the types of conversations that you want to hear. Take notes and create a tool to help you clarify these features. (Some rough ideas for such tools are in Chapter 5.) Observe and record conversations and use the tool to evaluate them.

Then work with colleagues in your grade level or content area to agree on what you want students to be able to do in conversations. You can synthesize multiple tools, if needed. Most of the tools should have conversation skills in some form. Then, in articulation meetings between grade levels, you can talk about the differences between them. In grade four, for example, students might be expected to build up both sides of an argument but not yet use multiple criteria to evaluate the strengths and weaknesses of each piece of evidence. The fifth- or sixth-grade tool might add these. Tools across grade levels might also differ in how many turns they expect, the length of the turns, and even the uses of certain types of language.

Choose and Adapt Approaches

A major influence on conversation work is the overall approach or approaches (i.e., the philosophy) used to design lessons and assessments. Even if an approach is not yet conversation rich, you can spot its potential and adapt it, as teachers often do. Conversation-poor approaches, however, tend to focus on transmission of knowledge from the text or teacher into students' heads without giving students opportunities to process the knowledge with others or do meaningful things with it. These approaches tend to emphasize teacher lectures, silent practice, and test-focused activities.

You can ask several questions about your curriculums' approach(es):

- Is the curriculum structured in such a way that students learn knowledge and skills for building up ideas?
- Can conversations help students succeed on tasks and assessments?
- Does the curriculum have rich opportunities for conversation? With some tweaking, is there some potential for productive conversations?
- Are the questions in the curriculum appropriate for conversations?

Often, teachers have their own approaches, and mixes of approaches, which can vary from that of the school and curriculum. Fortunately, some approaches can be adapted in various ways to support conversation development and content learning over time. I include two here. And based on my observations of their use in classrooms, I make a handful of suggestions for improving conversations within them.

Workshop Models

Workshop lessons tend to start with a minilesson in which the teacher models what students are supposed to learn or improve. Usually this is a reading or writing strategy that students will practice in their workshop time. One adaptation is modeling a conversation skill that students then practice in their workshop time. Before they talk, you can emphasize that the purpose of a workshop is to build the best, biggest, and strongest ideas possible using the strategy that they saw you model in the minilesson; the purpose is not just to practice an isolated strategy. I have also seen workshop groups have success when they split into pairs at times to have conversations about the ideas they are working on.

Project-Based Learning

Project-based learning, or PBL, is when students work on a project that engages them in answering a complex question or in solving a meaningful problem over time (e.g., one to eighteen weeks). The final product is usually some kind of report, presentation (often to authentic audiences), or simulation. Students need to use various sources in their research, including articles and primary sources. Students might need to interview key people or create surveys. In science, they might need to do an experiment or observe different phenomena. Some nonnegotiable design elements of PBL tend to include

- using multiple academic skills;
- reading multiple genres.;
- choosing their topic and how to communicate their final results;
- collaboration;
- multiple methods of communication (writing, oral speaking, visual presentations, publishing, etc.).

Now, a student could just choose a project, work by himself the whole time, and get a decent grade on the final product. But in PBL the journey, or process, is just as important. If the student didn't engage in conversations with anyone, he missed out on some important (but not often visible) learning. The final product, even if it received an A grade, could have been even better with conversational learning, and likely could have made a much more lasting change in the student's mind. And had he interacted with others, he might have helped them improve their learning as well. Remember, this is a new learning paradigm and culture for many students: moving away from the self-focused game of school to the collaborative and engaging building of ideas.

PBL offers rich opportunities for students to build up ideas with conversations. Yet in many PBL settings, more can be done to improve conversations as well as get the most out of them. True, good things can happen from giving students more agency and time for engaging in learning projects, but the extra work on developing conversation skills can pay off in a big way. Some ways to improve conversations in PBL are included in Table 6.5.

SUGGESTED ADAPTATION	EXAMPLE
Remind students that answering a big question (or an inquiry) or solving a big problem requires extensive building up of important ideas, and this means having different types of conversations at different stages of the project (initial, middle, and final).	For a project focused on creating a museum exhibit on the Silk Road, students used a semantic map organizer. In the center they put the main idea to be built up by visitors. Initial conversations focused on what they needed to research; middle conversations focused on using feedback to improve the clarity and organization of the exhibit; final conversations focused on what they learned in the project.
Have a model project that you use to model research and conversation skills. Before a model conversation, prepare your partner (likely a student) ahead of time for what you want to show the class through your conversation (e.g., clarifying, supporting, valuing partner responses, listening, building).	Throughout students' work on science projects focused on electricity and magnetism, their teacher modeled conversations with a volunteer partner on the topic of how motors work. She provided the partner with sample clarify and support questions beforehand and stopped the conversations at times to highlight the skills being used.
Create prompts that push students to practice the critical thinking needed for the project. Often modeling and prompts will include skills such as evaluating, using criteria, applying ideas to life, and recognizing bias.	In history research projects focused on the Industrial Revolution in Europe, the teacher prompted with, *Converse about how you will evaluate the credibility of web-based sources that you will use. What criteria will you use? Converse about the importance of your topic. What makes evidence strong and weak in your project?*
Have students self-assess their conversations using tools similar to those in Chapter 5.	In a high school English class, the teacher had students create their own self-assessment tool as a class. They could add one or two extra features to it, if they wanted, to personalize it. After each conversation (about *Hamlet*), they used the tool to evaluate how well they helped to build up the ideas they were working on.

Table 6.5 Examples of ways to improve conversations in project-based learning

Conclusion

Shifting to more conversation-based learning is a big challenge. It is not a quick fix with a few easy steps or a scripted curriculum. It takes a lot of time, patience, and willingness to get messy in the trenches of authentic learning. But it's well worth the efforts and risks when we see students who are more excited to learn, have better relationships with peers, learn content in more robust and lasting ways, and blossom into people who see the value of connecting with others throughout life.

Lastly, I want to thank you for your commitment to improving the learning and lives of our students. Our students deserve the best opportunities to learn in the short time they spend with us. Conversations are one way to provide such opportunities. Please feel free to contact me with any questions, successes, and insights that emerge in this important work.

Appendices

IDEA

Clarify

Support

Clarify

Support

Clarify

Support

Support

Clarify

Clarify

Support

Clarify

Support

Clarify

Support

Support

Clarify

Clarify

Support

Appendix A: Building Ideas Visual

Next Steps with Academic Conversations: New Ideas for Improving Learning Through Classroom Talk by Jeff Zwiers. © 2019. Stenhouse Publishers.

Argument Scale

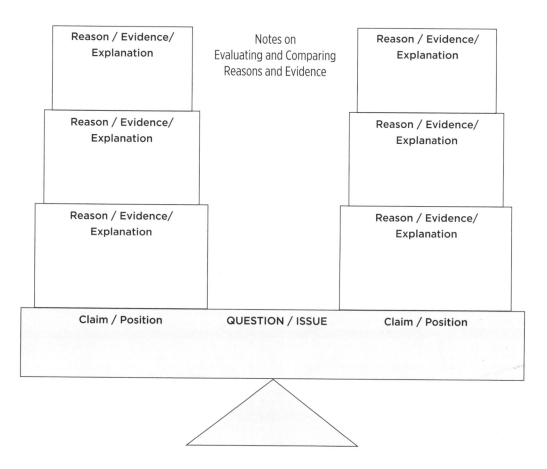

Appendix B: Two-Dimensional Argument Scale

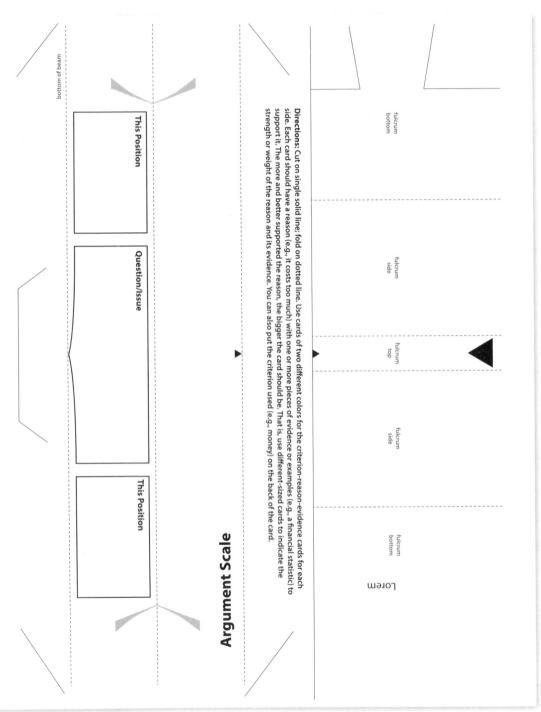

Directions: Cut on single solid line; fold on dotted line. Use cards of two different colors for the criterion-reason-evidence cards for each side. Each card should have a reason (e.g., it costs too much) with one or more pieces of evidence or examples (e.g., a financial statistic) to support it. The more and better supported the reason, the bigger the card should be. That is, use different-sized cards to indicate the strength or weight of the reason and its evidence. You can also put the criterion used (e.g., money) on the back of the card.

Argument Scale

This Position

Question/Issue

This Position

bottom of beam

fulcrum bottom

fulcrum side

fulcrum top

fulcrum side

fulcrum bottom

Lorem

Appendix C: Three-Dimensional Argument Scale

Next Steps with Academic Conversations: New Ideas for Improving Learning Through Classroom Talk by Jeff Zwiers. © 2019. Stenhouse Publishers.

	WELL	OK	NEED TO IMPROVE
I thought about how buildable the initial idea(s) that I or my partner posed.			
I clarified meanings and asked my partner to clarify, when needed or when in doubt.			
I supported ideas with examples and evidence and asked my partner for support when needed.			
We stayed focused on building an idea (or on both ideas, one after the other, if an argument).			
I valued my partner's ideas and showed with my body and eyes that I was listening.			

Appendix D: Sample Self-Assessment Tool

QUESTIONS	NOTES FOR FEEDBACK
How well did the students build up each idea and follow the prompt?	
How well did they use examples from the text? Did they explain the evidence?	
How well did they evaluate and compare the evidence on both sides?	
How hard did they try to explain their thoughts to one another?	
How much or how well did they use academic thinking?	

Appendix E: Sample Peer Assessment Tool

	FEATURES	RATINGS / NOTES
PREWRITE, CONVERSATION, AND POSTWRITE	Pose one or more relevant and buildable idea(s)	
	Support idea(s) with evidence, examples, explanations (accurate content)	
	Clarify idea(s) and terms (if needed)	
	Disciplinary thinking (cause-effect, interpret, perspective, bias, analyze . . .)	
	Language use (vocabulary, grammar, organization)	
	If it's an argument: evaluate and compare ideas to choose strongest/heaviest	
CONVERSATION	Build on one another's turns and take appropriate turns	
	Value each other's ideas	
	Nonverbal communication	

Appendix F: Sample Write-Converse-Write Assessment Tool

Ask your partner to clarify
_____
(Why, How . . .)

Refer to the text

Ask for evidence or an example to support the idea

Paraphrase what your partner said

Agree on a definition of
_____

Explain how and how well the evidence supports the idea

Encourage your partner to talk more
(and give time)

Show you are listening with eyes, nods, posture, etc.

Pose an alternative idea and start to build it up

Keep building up the first idea

Stay focused on the conversation purpose or prompt

Appendix G: Examples of Silent Coaching Cards

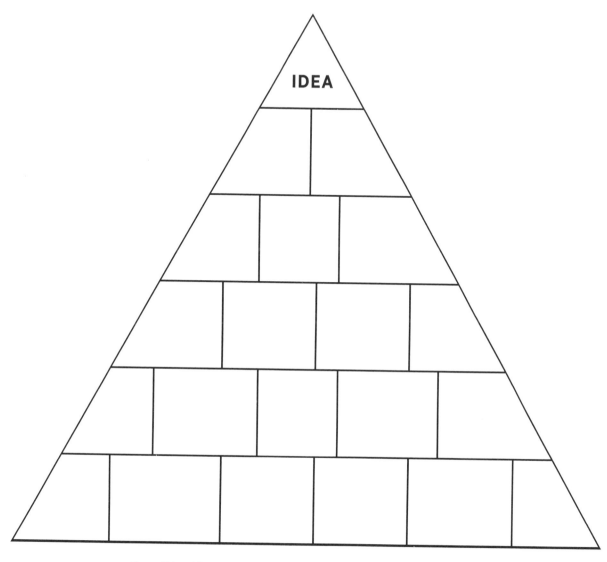

IDEA

C = Clarify, S = Support, E = Evaluate, V = Value

Appendix H: Sample Visual Organizer for Third Observer Notes (Building an Idea)

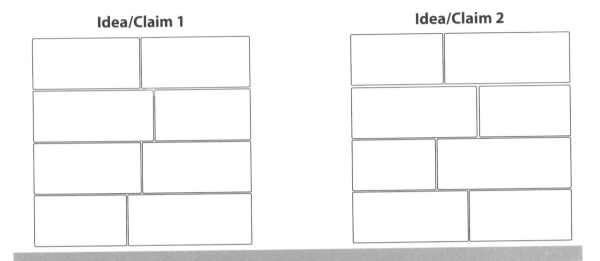

Idea/Claim 1

Idea/Claim 2

Sample Codes: C = Clarify, S = Support, E = Evaluate, V = Value

Appendix I: Sample Visual Organizer for Third Observer Notes (Argument)

References

Baker, A., P. J. Jensen, and D. A. Kolb. 2002. *Conversational Learning: An Experiential Approach to Knowledge Creation*. Westport, CT: Quorum Books.

Beck, I. L., M. G. McKeown, and L. Kucan. 2013. *Bringing Words to Life: Robust Vocabulary Instruction*. 2nd ed. New York: Guilford Press.

California State Board of Education. 2017. "United States History and Geography: Making a New Nation." In *California History-Social Science Framework*. Grade Five. Sacramento: California Department of Education. https://www.cde.ca.gov/ci/hs/cf/documents/hssfwchapter8.pdf.

Common Core State Standards. 2019a. "English Language Arts Standards—Reading: Informational Test—Grade 7." CCSS.ELA-LITERACY.RI.7.9. http://www.corestandards.org/ELA-Literacy/RI/7/.

———. 2019b. "English Language Arts Standards—Speaking & Listening—Grade 9–10." CCSS.ELA-LITERACY.SL.9-10.3. http://www.corestandards.org/ELA-Literacy/SL/9-10/.

———. 2019c. "English Language Arts Standards—Writing—Grade 3." CCSS.ELA-LITERACY.W.3.1. http://www.corestandards.org/ELA-Literacy/W/3/.

———. 2019d. "Grade 4—Measurement & Data." CCSS.MATH.CONTENT.4.MD.C.7. http://www.corestandards.org/Math/Content/4/MD/.

_____. 2019e. "Grade 7—Ratios & Proportional Relationships." CCSS.MATH. CONTENT.7.RP.A.2.A. http://www.corestandards.org/Math/Content/7/RP.

_____. 2019f. "High School Algebra: Reasoning with Equations & Inequalities." CCSS.MATH.CONTENT.HSA.REI.C.6. http://www.corestandards.org/ Math/Content/HSA/REI.

Daniels, H. 2002 . *Literature Circles: Voice and Choice in Book Clubs and Reading Groups.* (2nd ed.). Portland, ME: Stenhouse.

Fountas, I. C., & Pinnell, G. S. 2001. *Guiding Readers and Writers: Teaching Comprehension, Genre, and Content Literacy.* Portsmouth, NH: Heinemann.

Grice, H. P. 1975. "Logic and Conversation." In *Speech Acts*, ed. P. Cole and J. L. Morgan. New York: Academic Press.

Hari, R., and M. V. Kujala. 2007. "Brain Basis of Human Social Interaction: From Concepts to Brain Imaging." *Physiological Reviews* 89 (2): 453–479.

Jimenez, F. 1997. *The Circuit.* Albuquerque: University of New Mexico Press.

Johnson, D. W., and R. T Johnson . 1994. "Structuring Academic Controversy." *Handbook of Cooperative Learning Methods* , ed. S. Sharan. Westport, CT: Greenwood.

Keyes, D. 1966. *Flowers for Algernon.* New York: Harcourt.

Moeller, V. J., and M. V. Moeller. 2001. *Socratic Seminars and Literature Circles for Middle and High School English.* Larchmont, NY: Eye on Education.

New York State Social Studies Framework. 2015. 11.7c. https://www. bpsgroverteacher.com/uploads/1/4/8/4/14847764/nys_social_studies_ framework_us_history.pdf.

Next Generation Science Standards. 2019a. "4-LS1 from Molecules to Organisms: Structures and Processes." NGSS 4-LS1-1. https://www. nextgenscience.org/dci-arrangement/4-ls1-molecules-organisms- structures-and-processes.

_____. 2019b. "MS-PS2-4 Motion and Stability: Forces and Interactions." NGSS-MS-PS2.4. https://www.nextgenscience.org/pe/ms-ps2-4-motion- and-stability-forces-and-interactions.

_____. 2019c. "MS-ESS2-3 Earth's Systems." NGSS-MS-ESS2-3. https://www. nextgenscience.org/pe/ms-ess2-3-earths-systems.

Raphael, T. E., S. Florio-Ruane, and M. George. 2001. *Language Arts* 79 (2): 159–168.

Singer, T. W., and J. Zwiers. 2016. "What Conversations Can Capture." Educational Leadership 73 (7).

Washington State Standards for Social Science: Grade 7. 2019. WashingtonState.G7.1.2.3. https://www.perma-bound.com/state-standards.do?state=WA&subject=social-studies&gradeLevel=7.

White, E. B. 1952. *Charlotte's Web*. New York: Harper & Brothers.

Zwiers, J., and M. Crawford. 2011. *Academic Conversations: Classroom Talk That Fosters Critical Thinking and Content Understandings*. Portland, ME: Stenhouse.

Recommended Resources

Cazden, C. 2001. *Classroom Discourse: The Language of Teaching and Learning*. Portsmouth, NH: Heinemann.

Chinn, C. A., and D. B. Clark. 2013. "Learning Through Collaborative Argumentation." In *The International Handbook of Collaborative Learning*, ed. C. E. Hmelo-Silver, C. A. Chinn, C. K. K. Chan, and A. O'Donnell. Educational Psychology Handbook Series. New York: Routledge/Taylor & Francis Group.

Edwards, D., and N. Mercer. 1993. *Common Knowledge: The Development of Understanding in the Classroom*. London: Routledge.

Felton, M., M. Garcia-Mila, C. Villarroel, and S. Gilabert. 2015. "Arguing Collaboratively: Argumentative Discourse Types and Their Potential for Knowledge Building." *British Journal of Educational Psychology* 85:372–386.

Gee, J. 1996. *Social Linguistics and Literacies: Ideology in Discourses*. London: Routledge Falmer.

Mehan, H. 1979. *Learning Lessons: Social Organization in the Classroom*. Cambridge, MA: Harvard University Press.

Mercer, N. 2000. *The Guided Construction of Knowledge: Talk Amongst Teachers and Learners*. Clevedon, England: Multilingual Matters.

Nichols, M. 2006. *Comprehension Through Conversation: The Power of Purposeful Talk in the Reading Workshop*. Portsmouth, NH: Heinemann.

Nystrand, M. 1997. *Opening Dialogue: Understanding the Dynamics of Language and Learning in the English Classroom.* New York: Teachers College Press.

Osborne, J. 2010. "Arguing to Learn in Science: The Role of Collaborative, Critical Discourse." *Science* 328 (5977): 463–466.

Toulmin, S. 2003. *The Uses of Argument.* Cambridge: Cambridge University Press.

Vygotsky, L. 1986. *Thought and Language.* Translated by A. Kozulin. Cambridge, MA: MIT Press.

Index

P

pair-shares, 163-165
paraphrase practice, 54-55
patterns
    looking for, 144-145
    sample assessment tool, looking for, 146
peer, self-assessment tools, 140-143
peer assessment tool, 141-143, 188
persuasive techniques, 68-69
Pinnell, G.S., 99
posing, conversation-worthy ideas, 48-52
    key words in envelope, 51-52
pro-con improvisation activity, 71-73
professional learning communities (PLC), 177
project-based learning (PBL), 179-180
prompts, 22-29
    effective, ineffective and, 24
    engaging, 23
    expectations, directions and, 23
    need to talk, 23
    standards and, 25-28
    strategies for creating, 25-29

R

Rapheal, Taffy E., 99
relevant ideas, 49
role-based improvisation conversations, 104
    activity, 79-82
rotating mini-jigsaw triads, 169-170

S

schoolwide systems, supports, 176-178
    choosing, adapting approaches to, 178
    conversational goals and, 177-178
    professional learning communities and, 177
    project-based learning and, 179-180
    schoolwide agreement regarding
        conversations and, 176-177
    workshop models and, 179
science conversations, 115-120
    designing experiments, interpreting data,
        116-117
    explaining scientific phenomena, 118-119
    science role-based, 119-120
self-assessment tool, sample, 140-141, 187
silent coaching cards, 171-172
    sample, 190
Singer, T.W., 135
skills, clarification, 52-54
socio-emotional skills, academic conversations
    and, 6-7
Socratic conversations, 102-103

speaking, focused, 17
standards, prompts , 25-28
structured academic controversies (SACs), 78-79
student pairing, grouping, 162-163
    clock partners, 162
supporting ideas
    back it up, 59
    evidence, non-evidence, 59
    evidence from own life, 57
    evidence from text, 56-57
    evidence from world, 57
    information gap cards, 61-62

T

take a side, convince three on fence activity,
    83-85
teacher supports, 155
thinking skills, 18-21
    language arts, 19
    science, 18
    social studies, history, 19
think-pair-shares, 163-165
three-dimensional argument scale, 186
turn-and-talks, 163-165
two-dimensional argument scale, 185

W

what, why information gap math cards, 109
workshop models, 179
write-converse-write assessment tool, 189
write-converse-write (WCW) protocol, 149-155
    analysis tool, 151
    procedure, 150-151
    sample, 152-153
writing, conversing
    describe, narrate information gap and, 99
    modified writing process and, 96-97
writing, conversing, and, 96-99

Z

Zwiers, J., 135
Zwiers, J. and M. Crawford, Academic
    Conversations, 1-2